BEING MISS AMERICA

Discovering
AMERICA

Mark Crispin Miller, Series Editor

This series begins with a startling premise—
that even now, more than two hundred years
since its founding, America remains a largely
undiscovered country with much of its amazing story yet to be told. In these books, some of
America's foremost historians and cultural critics bring to light episodes in our nation's history that have never been explored. They offer
fresh takes on events and people we thought we
knew well and draw unexpected connections
that deepen our understanding of our national
character.

Kate Shindle

BEING MISS AMERICA

BEHIND THE RHINESTONE CURTAIN

University of Texas Press

AUSTIN

Requests for permission to reproduce material from this work should
be sent to:
    Permissions
    University of Texas Press
    P.O. Box 7819
    Austin, TX 78713-7819
    http://utpress.utexas.edu/index.php/rp-form

♾ The paper used in this book meets the minimum requirements of
ANSI/NISO Z39.48 1992 (R1997) (Permanence of Paper).

Cataloging data is available upon request from the Library of Congress.
Library of Congress Control Number: 2014936789
ISBN 978-0-292-73921-5 (cloth : alk. paper)
doi:10.7560/739215

To the millions of people who change the world
every day, without the recognition or power
of the Miss America crown.

To my family, for impressing upon me the magic of
Miss America and supporting me as I chased that
goal—especially my dad, Gordon Shindle,
the most ethical person I know.

And to all the volunteers who unselfishly
make Miss America happen, particularly
Fran Skinner-Lewis, who introduced me to myself
and continues to show me that the world is
so much bigger than I think it is.

CONTENTS

PROLOGUE

When people hear that I was Miss America, their first question is almost always the same. "What was that like?"

The sentence doesn't always come out the same way, of course. Those who are awed by it—who grew up knowing Miss America as annual destination television on the second Saturday in September—almost always emphasize the last word. "What was that *like*?" they ask, their eyes gleaming with wistfulness and excitement and a little bit of envy. To them, you are royalty in disguise, whether you're at a black-tie event or in the locker room at your gym. The very idea that you may have been masquerading as a normal civilian is baffling; to them, Miss America is something that should be worn on one's sleeve. It is the ultimate of ultimate achievements.

And then there's the other camp. The camp that makes a predictable set of assumptions about you as soon as they hear that phrase. *Miss America*. Before you even open your mouth, they've pegged you as some kind of inferior being— vain, airheaded, or worse; the kind of smart girl who has become a sellout and traded on her looks instead of working her way up the ladder like everyone else. And in that case, the emphasis changes and is accompanied by a knowing little sneer: "What was *that* like?"

There is a third group. It is very, very small. It's made up of a few people who have been around the pageant for a long time, a handful of journalists (Frank Deford comes to mind), one or two very smart publicists, about half of the former Miss Americas, and a few dozen of their closest friends and family members. And then, occasionally, if you spend enough time as an ex–Miss America, you run into extra, random members of this third group.

These are the ones who just ask you the question with no dramatic emphasis on any particular word. When they lean in and ask, "What was that like?" it's because they really want to know. Because they recognize that along with being one of the nation's oldest not-for-profit institutions, Miss America is among our most complex. They have watched, sometimes peripherally, as this tradition has white-knuckled its way down the cultural ladder, rung by rung by painful rung. They may have a certain amount of reverence for the crown, but not so much that they can't see it with clear and pragmatic eyes. And they are curious as to how it must feel to be a thinking person living inside the mythology of Miss America.

It is the third group—those I have met and, especially, those I have not—for whom I primarily write this book.

BEING MISS AMERICA

Part One

FLAPPERS AND SCHOLARS
AND CROWNS, OH MY!

ONE

It doesn't hit me for almost a month after I win that I am, in fact, Miss America.

When I was a kid, I was a pretty good student. A little prone to procrastination, perhaps, but good nonetheless. Apparently I grew up with undiagnosed ADHD, which might explain why I had problems focusing on things—homework, cleaning my dresser drawers—unless I was faced with pressing and non-negotiable deadlines. But damn, could I write a great essay the night before it was due.

Like all kids, though, I didn't always do things right. Occasionally, a punitive writing exercise found its way onto my to-do list, the kind intended to drill your priorities into your head by way of your aching fingers. The kind that makes kids shudder with boredom before they even pick up the pen. More than anything, it takes an exercise like this to get me to digest that I've actually won the crown.

I am in a hotel room, like I suddenly always am. This one is in Washington, DC, mere weeks after the acquisition of my sparkly new hat. And just as I did years ago in school, I have an assignment. This time I have to write "Kate Shindle, Miss America 1998." Six hundred times. On eight-by-ten glossy color pictures of my own head.

Signing autographs, as it happens, is already my least favorite part of the gig. This particular batch, on this particular day, is for the people back home. My adopted home, that is, near the Chicago suburbs where I've just finished my junior year at Northwestern University. Every year, the new Miss America has a homecoming in the state she's represented at the big event. The director of the Miss Illinois Pageant (of whom I've spent the past three months completely terrified, but who will eventually become a best friend/ big sister/surrogate mom) has by far the smartest marketing mind I've ever come across. She actually gets the city of Oakbrook Terrace, a largely corporate suburb looking to heighten its visibility, to pony up something like $100,000 a year for the honor of hosting the Miss Illinois Pageant. It's brilliant—much of the country is struggling to hang on to sponsors and donors and scholarships, and Fran has cracked the code of how to pitch the whole damn thing in a cash-generating way.

The downside for me, at the moment, is that everyone who has rallied or provided support for the state pageant is foaming at the mouth with excitement that Miss Illinois has brought home the national crown. And what do they want? An autographed picture. For the really big contributors, these will be made into plaques, and I will personally be on hand to present them. Kate Shindle, Miss America 1998. Kate Shindle, Miss America 1998. For Cynthia, the trainer who spent dozens of unpaid hours whipping my ass into shape and schooling me on the virtues of slow-cooked oatmeal. Kate Shindle, Miss America 1998. For Karen, who taught me the fine cosmetic line between "stage face" and "drag queen." Kate Shindle, Miss America 1998. For Linda, who traveled all over the state with me and tried not to laugh while I agonized over what fraction of a PowerBar would give me just enough energy to get through my second workout of the day. For Curtis, who orchestrated my music for the talent competition, and Dominic, who staged it. Kate Shin-

4

dle, Miss America 1998. For Robin, who donated and/or created thousands of dollars' worth of wardrobe for just about every phase of competition. For the mayor of Oakbrook Terrace. For the people who own the Drury Lane Theatre. For Costa's Greek Restaurant, which provides food for Miss Illinois Week. For the president of Northwestern University. For Kurt, my voice teacher. For Joel, who made a valiant (and nearly successful) effort to teach me how to put my hair up with little pieces carelessly tendrilling their way out. Kate Shindle, Miss America 1998. For Chuck, the Chicago Bulls executive who snagged me a pair of Michael Jordan's championship-series sneakers to wear in the Miss America Boardwalk Parade, where the fans scream "Show us your shoes!" and every contestant wants hers to be the coolest. To the Miss Illinois judges, who told me on the night they selected me that they thought I might "sneak in there" in Atlantic City. To Carol and Ken and Jackie and Marjorie and Sandy and Chip and Kelli and . . . I start to lose track of all the people who practiced interview skills with me, encouraged me, helped me to pack my thirteen suitcases, in which every single item had to be labeled "Illinois," at—characteristically—the very, very last minute. If I were to look at the video of the night I won the pageant, I would see myself joyfully waving to them as I spot them in the Convention Hall audience. Yeah, yeah. Waving is easy. Especially when you can't quite feel your body. Signing six hundred pictures is work. Kate Shindle, Miss America 1998. Kate Shindle, Miss America 1998.

The first time I hear these words, of course—the actual moment when I win the crown—I can't fathom ever getting tired of them. Miss America. I have powered through two weeks of appearances, competitions, interviews, and the like with the other fifty representatives (1997 is the year that Washington, DC, has returned to the lineup), and been part of each group that advances to the next level on the final Saturday night. I stand in the middle of the top five as we all clutch hands. Unlike the rest of the evening, though, this part of the affair is the time you don't want to hear your name called. Miss California is called as fourth runner-up. (Don't say Illinois!) Miss Arizona is third runner-up. (Don't say Illinois!) Miss Mississippi gets second runner-up. And then it's just me and Miss North Carolina, a stunning blonde who looks like a contemporary Grace Kelly and has brought the house down with her talent performance. But right before they announce her name as first runner-up, I just know. Later, pageant officials will tell me that the final ballot wasn't even close, and that the point spread between me and the rest of the top five was the biggest in recent memory. Later, I will find out that my interview—the first competition of the week—was strong enough to carry me through the rest of the proceedings, and that the celebrity judges, who watch videos of the top ten interviews on Saturday afternoon and then judge the finals, had to take an unscheduled break because one member of the panel was so emotional after my closing statement about the AIDS quilt. Later, there will be reasons that make logical, numerical sense.

But in this moment, the moment just before they make the announcement, there's an awareness that simply washes over me like a tidal wave. Becoming Miss America will change the whole course of my life for a very long time, if not forever. And I believe that when a change of this magnitude is barreling toward you, the universe gives you a heads-up. Suddenly, I'm no longer hoping that they'll call Miss North Carolina as first runner-up. I'm certain of it.

The next bit can't be described as anything but surreal. There's a voice in my head—my own voice, in a tone I would use to recite a grocery list—calmly walking me through the necessary steps. Bend your knees so Tara can pin the crown on. Take the scepter. Oh, there's the stage manager, at the end of the runway, waving her white-gloved hands to catch your attention. Walk toward her. Duh, you've been watching this thing all your life, you know about the part with the runway! *On camera, of course, it doesn't look anything like this; I just look like a girl who's really excited that she's the new Miss America. But living it is an out-of-body experience. And then I'm off, to a press conference and a photo shoot and to speak to the other contestants and their families, to a sponsor party with a mile-long line of strangers congratulating me. Through the Claridge lobby, packed to the rafters with familiar and unfamiliar faces, cheering. Up to my new hotel suite, to visit with family, then pile, fully dressed, into the (empty) hot tub with my school friends, and eventually, sleep for a couple of hours. And then awake again, prancing awkwardly in the ocean for photographers, changing into my interview suit for another press conference, condensing my belongings into a couple of suitcases, then climbing into a stretch limo and speeding up the Garden State Parkway to Manhattan.*

To say that my life has changed drastically is both an understatement and an overstatement. The overstatement part is simple. I sort of just feel like the same old drama-geek me; I just have different stuff to do now. But the understatement—whoa. I have flown first class for the first time ever—right now, in 1997, Miss America never flies coach. I have no problem with this. I hate that discriminatory little curtain they pull between the sections of the plane, but I like the free warm nuts and hot towels enough to get over it.

I feel like I've been on almost every TV show people watch. Today, Good Morning America, The Tonight Show, Regis and Kathie Lee, *and a brand-new show called* The View. *I have listened as the media and the public—mostly on television and various op-ed pages—analyze nearly everything about my recent win. I have visited designer showrooms, where clothes were practically shoveled at me; I have slept in hotel suites with (can you believe it?) multiple bathrooms. I've been invited to sing the National Anthem at Northwestern's Homecoming game, and for the Bulls' championship ring ceremony. I have gone on a date with possibly the most gorgeous guy I've ever met, who would never have looked at me twice before Miss America . . . and I have also gotten flowers from my first boyfriend, who once broke up with me by just not really calling anymore. I have launched my platform issue—the public service project every contestant is required to develop—with a speech on the lawn of the Capitol in Washington, DC.*

In the meantime, my mom has gamely moved all of my college-appropriate stuff (everything from holey sweatpants to the tattered running shoes that carried me around campus this past summer) out of my little apartment in Evanston and back home to New Jersey. I won't be spending more than a handful of nights in any one place between now and next year's pageant, so there's really no sense in keeping an apartment at school. In my absence, my quirky engineering grad student roommate will be using the empty living room to practice for her ballroom dancing competitions, because I guess it makes more sense than just getting another couch. I haven't seen my friends for weeks—and even then, only the ones who were intrepid enough to make the 1,000-mile drive from Chicago to Atlantic City to watch the competition in person. I know that people all over campus have gotten calls from tabloids digging for dirt, and some have been offered money to tell some scandalous secrets about me—the press, it seems, is forever crossing its ink-stained fingers for another Vanessa Williams. One of my friends told off the caller in spectacular fashion; another buried the only photograph with the ability to cause mild controversy. Thank you, Daniel and Kevin.

I'm on pace to travel 20,000 miles every month, crisscrossing the nation in an almost random pattern to speak to students, lobby legislators, raise money for nonprofits, and generally spread the message that AIDS is bad, we know how to stay safe from it, and given the infection stats both domestically and abroad, we'd better hustle.

The downside of this particular life moment is something

I haven't anticipated: the likelihood that those I meet, those who observe me from afar—and, most troubling, those I already know—will feel compelled to decide who I am on the basis of a few facts and the trivia they access on the rapidly evolving Internet. One minute I'm a gawky, showtune-loving, dean's list student at a top university. I have treated Miss America like I would any other goal; in the face of impossible odds, I am ferociously competitive and laser-focused. Of course I get my act together and go to Atlantic City planning to win. Then someone puts a crown on my head, and all bets were off.

Suddenly, people make wild assumptions based on very little information. Suddenly, I will never again just be Kate Shindle; I will always carry the mantle—and, as it turns out, the baggage that comes with it—of Miss America's complicated history. And brains versus looks. And, you know, most of the nation's ideas about womanhood and femininity and stuff. A few weeks from now, on my short Christmas break, there will be a well-intentioned but somewhat awkward reception at my South Jersey elementary school, where neighbors, family friends, teachers, and anyone else who happens to be nearby will line up for autographs and photos with me. Even some of those people will start to see me as an institution rather than a person they've known since kindergarten or earlier. But later that week, I'll watch Northwestern play in the Citrus Bowl (in which we get schooled by Tennessee) and sit slack-jawed as I see, for the first time, what Peyton Manning can do with a football. And in Knoxville in a few months, I'll drop hints to the limo driver—and anyone else who will listen—until I get to sit in Phil Fulmer's office and talk to Manning about school, and football, and his little brother at Ole Miss. So it's a bit hypocritical to complain about one aspect of this new identity while simultaneously learning how to leverage it.

I have been called courageous, a trailblazer, the first socially relevant Miss America ever, fat, thin, beautiful, hand-

some, ugly, talented, untalented, inspiring, infuriating, deserving, undeserving. The media have parked for days outside my parents' house, rung the doorbell and phone relentlessly, gone through the trash cans. At some point in the near future, Howard Stern will apparently call me a whore, although I will only hear about it secondhand. When you make AIDS your cause, people project all kinds of things onto you. In reality, I am the furthest thing from a whore, to a degree that's almost embarrassing. But I don't want that to get out, because I'm pretty sure the high school students I'm going to face this year will listen more attentively to my safer-sex message if I don't run all over the country disclosing that I am, in fact, about as pure as the driven snow. It's a conundrum: travel the country telling people to use condoms, while I myself have never had cause to make some of the choices I advocate.

Even in the late 1990s, after Miss America has been pronounced dead, extinct, irrelevant more times than anyone can probably count, I am newsworthy. Children climb over each other at assemblies to touch me. Or the crown. I can't always tell which.

I've read that Princess Diana—who at this point in history has been dead about six weeks—had trouble reconciling who she was as a human with the royal image she had to live up to. I'm starting to get it.

Kate Shindle, Miss America 1998. Kate Shindle, Miss America 1998.

TWO

In March of 2011, about six weeks after the Miss America Organization (MAO) celebrated its ninetieth anniversary, eighty-seven-year-old Jean Bartel, Miss America 1943, died.

Former Miss Americas are a unique breed. They are achievers, certainly; even the least type A's among the group are generally pretty driven women. They are competitive—and not just because most have spent years pushing themselves into the position of Miss America, but because after that tremendous accomplishment comes and goes, many find that there is no off switch for their considerable ambition. And so any gathering of former Miss Americas rapidly and invariably turns into its own contest. Who among these women is the most beautiful, most intelligent, most accomplished, most altruistic, *most ideal* of the "ideal" that Bert Parks used to sing about? It's a never-ending race with no official winner.

And yet, for all this internal jockeying for position, it is also a group of women who are generally affectionate—toward one another and toward the program that has provided them with a lasting identity. By and large, they are capital-L Ladies. Most are either Southern or have taken on

a Southern-type identity of what it means to be feminine—
a product, no doubt, of the fact that Miss America has always been more deeply in demand in the Bible Belt than
anywhere else, and a girl's got to learn how to walk softly
and keep the big stick hidden.

Some are saccharine, some a little dippy, some snarky.
Like clockwork, there is one from each decade who seems
never to have taken the crown off—she's either leveraged
it into an extremely successful career or she's still trying
to white-knuckle her fifteen minutes. In general, though,
they're pretty kind. The Miss Americas are a sorority of
sorts; it is not at all rare for them to begin a group e-mail
message with "My dearest sisters" and conclude it with
a prayer or a request for prayers. Although some of these
women barely know one another, they share a steely bond
forged by the Miss America experience, an experience that
requires a young woman to take on a mantle that grows
both more storied and more burdensome with each passing year. Uneasy lies the head that wears the crown, indeed; it doesn't help that the crown itself seems to get exponentially weightier with the passage of time. Most of the
young women who strive to become Miss America see it as
the public sees it: as a dream, a wish fulfillment that guar-
antees one will be respected, praised, and lifted up as an
example of all that is right about young American women.
Little do they know what they're actually getting into if
they win. Decades of stereotypes, expectations, scandal,
myths, media scrutiny, public skepticism, and questionable
leadership choices have made actually *being* Miss America
nearly impossible. That kind of shared crucible makes for
some serious camaraderie.

And so, when the news broke that Jean Bartel was gone,
the Miss Americas flooded each other's in-boxes with sym-
pathy and prayers and shared reminiscences of the woman
they had known. They expressed sadness and shock; having just seen her in Las Vegas, no one could believe that she

had passed so quickly. Mostly, they said things like "she will be missed" and "such a precious gem" and "a legend, a beauty, an example."

I had a different reaction. I had met Jean; I liked her very much. But mostly, the death of Jean Bartel kind of made me cranky.

I never planned to be a black sheep Miss America. I'm still not exactly sure how it happened. I do know that in a sea of genteel, Southernish women, I'm the one who grew up in New Jersey and went to school in Chicago. I do know that I have a very difficult time holding my tongue when something is unfair or when people are being treated badly. I can clearly see the difference between taking the high road and being a doormat. And I have watched Miss America slowly and painfully fall apart in a way that would have had longtime director Lenora Slaughter rolling over in her grave.

Jean's death hit home for me because, in most of the ways that matter, she was the first one to make Miss America mean something. There are a couple of different versions of the story (a common theme in this mostly oral history), but the most widely accepted is the version where Jean—then the current Miss America—brought Slaughter a crazy idea that she and her sorority sisters had dreamed up: in addition to the screen test and fur coat and whatever else Miss America received as prizes, she should also get a college scholarship.

Today, the Miss America Organization frequently claims to be the largest provider of scholarships for women in the world. Each year, it makes available about $45 million in cash and in-kind scholarships to young women ages 17 to 24. All because Jean Bartel chatted over tea with some women her own age and almost single-handedly transformed the pageant. She saw beyond the borderline-smarmy boardwalk parade featuring "amateur" and "professional" women, bathing suits and tape measures, and handed the leadership the keys to the legitimacy kingdom. It is a testament to her significance that both the *Huffington Post* and *Jezebel*, two unlikely sources of praise for pageants, lauded her following her death. She was a transformational Miss America.

And that's really the reason I was mad. It struck me that her death brought things full circle, at what was the end of a very long era. An era in which the young women beneath the crown were able to push the pageant to do things that would lift up their successors. An era in which the pageant brass knew enough to steal a good idea when they heard one. An era in which no one would've said the pageant was perfect—its idiosyncrasies are the very things that make it endearing—but in which it crept closer and closer to the edge of cultural relevance. And when it got right up to the precipice, instead of jumping, it took fifteen steps backward.

And so, while I also sent along my best wishes to Jean's family (after all, when you're an ex–Miss America, appropriateness almost always wins the day), I sat and stewed. And I looked at what the pageant had become, and wondered what Jean Bartel would think.

It started as a stunt.

There are plenty of stories of Miss America's history, many of them colored by opinions and agendas on all sides. But one thing that nearly everyone agrees on is this: if the hoteliers and assorted businessmen of Atlantic City hadn't wanted to wring one more week out of the bustling tourist season, Miss America probably wouldn't exist in the first place.

It's more complicated than that, of course. In America in 1920, when the seeds of women's rights were being sowed by a growing minority, the definition of femininity was ever-changing. Scarlett O'Hara was clinging to life somewhere in the Deep South, and the career woman-slash-supermom was yet to be discovered. In an era where the role of women in the United States morphed at a previously unheard-of speed, the flapper—sexy, brazen, smart, and unafraid to dance on a table while people were watching—was born. With the First World War over, she cast off her Victorian corset, bobbed her hair, and stayed out all night smoking cigarettes and drinking gin at speakeasies. She represented a new type of female freedom, a bold working girl in a consumer-driven society. She glamorized deviant behavior and traumatized those who believed that women should aspire to (a) provide good homes for their families and (b) avoid scandal at all costs. The flapper didn't hide from scandal; in general, she ran straight into its appealingly dangerous clutches. And by doing so, she laid the groundwork for what was about to happen in Atlantic City. The flapper couldn't survive just anywhere—even Zelda Fitzgerald had to move to New York to complete her transformation—and as she restlessly searched for a home base that would embrace her progressive identity, she threw off seedlings that would blossom into various paradigms of femininity. The seedling that landed in Atlantic City, which in 1921 was teetering between the traditional and the risqué, grew into the flapper's prim cousin. They would call her Miss America.

In 1921, a group of businessmen in Atlantic City (then a luxurious summer vacation resort) came up with a gimmick that capitalized on the craze for sexy, independent womanhood. Not for nothing, it also served to extend the summer season by one additional week. They created the Fall Frolic, a festival which included the Atlantic City Bathing Beauty Contest and was scheduled for the weekend after Labor Day. A hundred thousand people showed up to watch eight contestants parade down the Boardwalk in their knee-length bathing costumes, culminating in the crowning of sixteen-year-old Margaret Gorman from Washington, DC. Her body, according to the *New York Times*, was "a 30-25-32 figure that was close to the flapper era ideal"—although, unlike some of her competitors, she was modest enough to wear her stockings on the beach.

The pageant's smashing financial success and massive popularity pretty much guaranteed that it would be repeated. But it was not without its detractors—a theme that would be increasingly familiar to Miss America's leadership in the decades to come. By 1923, when attendance at the pageant swelled to 300,000, the business leaders and newspapers that had sparked its creation were growing uneasy; ironically, they were nervous about Miss America's effect on Atlantic City's image. Women's groups protested against this public display, which they viewed as alternately immoral and exploitative. It was the beginning of a long and fascinating push-and-pull between Miss America and ideals of twentieth-century femininity.

For a time, the protesters won. Even though the pageant eliminated the "professional" (intended for actresses and models) category in 1923 (the same year that Mary Katherine Campbell became the only woman who would ever win the pageant twice, prompting numerous show business offers, including one from Florenz Ziegfield himself), conservative groups began to push back hard. After all, it was not only the era of the liberated young woman, but also the era of Prohibition—an indication that advocates of enforced morality were not going to lose their country to purveyors of beaded fringe. The year 1925 brought what appeared to be substantive allegations (later proven false) that the pageant was fixed to ensure the win of California's Fay Lanphier, which added fuel to the moralists' fire. In 1927, Norma Smallwood turned the Miss America title into a career. Today, she is remembered more for leveraging her fame into sponsorships than for the fact that she remains the only Native American woman ever to grab the Miss America crown.

For all of these reasons—protesters, disorganization, and certainly the pall cast by the economic crash that was barreling toward America—the pageant was discontinued. There would be no Miss America in 1928. Or, for that matter, in 1929, 1930, 1931, or 1932.

After a hiatus of a few years, and with the aftereffects of the Great Depression still hanging over most of the country, Director General Armand T. Nichols pushed hard for Atlantic City to revive its biggest publicity event. Copycat pageants were starting to spring up in other seaside towns (particularly troublesome was neighboring Wildwood, New Jersey). By most accounts, however, the 1933 effort was poorly organized and a financial and public-relations disaster. While professional women were allowed to compete for the Bathing Beauty titles (and an RKO screen test was among the prizes to be awarded), pageant organizers made it clear that they were not looking for a showgirl. The major controversy (if one doesn't count Miss Maine and Miss New Hampshire forgetting their bathing suits, Miss New York State passing out during the judging because of a bad toothache, or Miss Oklahoma dropping out for an emergency appendectomy) was the disqualification of three contestants alleged not to live in the states they were representing. Just before the pageant, officials announced to the assembled media that *four* young women had actually been disqualified: Misses Iowa, Illinois, and Idaho for residency issues, and Miss Arkansas for being married. As if that weren't enough for one Saturday in September, Miss New York City (who had beaten out ten thousand rivals at Madison Square Garden) quit a few hours before the finals, "saying that the pageant was not on the up and up." In the end, the crown went to Miss Connecticut, Marion Bergeron, a squeaky-clean fifteen-year-old blues singer who attended convent school—and who returned to her school a year later to be told that the nuns felt she "had had entirely too much undue publicity" to continue her education there.

The year 1933 was also noteworthy for the friction that began to develop between the Miss America organizers and the pageant's home in Atlantic City. Director General Nichols dangled the idea that he had received offers to stage the festivities in other cities, and that he was disappointed in the lack of support from the Atlantic City Chamber of Commerce. As for Mayor Harry Bacharach, he speculated that when all was said and done, no money had been made by that year's pageant. It was a tension that would continue for decades to come, as idea men, money men, and legislators fought for the three C's: control, capital, and credit.

And just like that, Miss America was dead again. There was no Atlantic City pageant in 1934, although Madison Square Garden gave it a shot, selecting a "Queen of American Beauty."

In 1935, however, the pageant got serious. Certain that Miss America was a cash cow waiting to happen, some new leaders stepped in, accompanied by one very interesting woman. According to the Miss America Organization, "Steel Pier owner Frank P. Gravatt and associate Eddie Corcoran enlisted the help of the Variety Club of Philadelphia to bring back Miss America. Corcoran hired Lenora S. Slaughter from the Chamber of Commerce in St. Petersburg, Florida, for a six-week stint that lasted thirty-two years. Her immediate goal was to build interest within Atlantic City itself. The Boardwalk Parade was brought back with 350,000 people in attendance. The 1920s pageant mascot, 'King Neptune,' also made a valiant return. Fifty-two contestants, representing eleven states and forty-one key cities, took part."

Lenora Slaughter, in particular, was a genteel Southern woman with big-picture ideas and big-city negotiating skills. When Eddie Corcoran died shortly after bringing her on, she grabbed the pageant by its nether regions and didn't let go for three decades. Miss America historian

Ric Ferentz once referred to her—and one suspects he was not the only individual to do this, nor the user of the most colorful language—as a classic "iron fist in a velvet glove." During her time with the pageant (her original title was "Executive Secretary," and despite her married status, she was always referred to as "Miss Slaughter"), she set out to convince skeptics and supporters alike that the pageant had been off the mark from the start.

Throughout her tenure, Slaughter fought a battle that can be summed up pretty simply, one that continues to this day and has never quite been won. Deserved or not, Miss America had already acquired something of a cheesecake image, and a mercenary one at that: young women cashing in on their anatomical blessings to win a prize, gain notoriety, even launch a career. There seem to be no indications that most of those involved in the event—the founding businessmen, the media, or the Hollywood executives who came calling—had much of a problem with that. Interestingly, just as the pageant's earliest detractors were women concerned with the image of American femininity, so too was the individual who pushed to transform Miss America into something more than the "right" measurements, hairstyle, and marketability potential.

"'First thing,'" she explained in Angela Saulino Osborne's 1995 book *Miss America: The Dream Lives On*, "'I had to get Atlantic City to understand that it couldn't just be a beauty contest.'" And did she ever. More than thirty years later, when Slaughter retired, she had almost single-handedly transformed Miss America into an aspirational icon for millions of girls and young women across the nation, a symbol of cultural respectability, an instant celebrity from the moment she was crowned, and the face of a wildly popular organization whose telecast drew as many eyeballs as any other event on television. She accomplished this by taking one deliberate step at a time: a college scholarship for the winner (unheard of when it was first initiated), a talent competition, a coterie of sponsors for the program, and a veritable army of volunteers to pull off the event each year. And not just any volunteers—in order to form the first Hostess Committee, for example, Slaughter focused her attention on Atlantic City high society, recruiting each "lady of the house" with potential to be a chaperone of sorts. In effect, she leveraged the credibility of the hostesses themselves to create an aura of sterling reputations for the contestants, and for Miss America herself.

Initially, Slaughter's success rested precariously on a house of cards. She faced her first challenge almost immediately upon her arrival in 1935. That year's winner, a high school dropout from Pittsburgh named Henrietta Leaver, found herself in a protracted battle with Frank Vittel, a renowned artist who had used her sittings (in which she consistently claimed that her grandmother was present, and that she had worn a bathing suit) to create a nude sculpture of her. Although she did not lose her Miss America title, she was not invited to crown her successor, since she had married during her year. Two years later, the 1937 winner (seventeen-year-old Bette Cooper) disappeared within hours of her crowning. According to the Miss America archives, "Bette, having second thoughts about her commitment, took off with her Pageant male chaperone, Frank Off, in a motor boat. The two floated around Atlantic City until the boardwalk crowds dispersed. No other contestant was crowned Miss America in her absence, though several participants from that year have made claim to the title throughout the decades. Bette lives a quiet life in Connecticut. A soft-spoken person of polite cordiality, Bette still refuses to talk to reporters, the Pageant staff and others about her involvement."

Despite these setbacks, however, Slaughter can reasonably be credited with substantial accomplishments during the early years of her tenure; first and foremost, she began running the pageant less like a garden party and more like a business. Under her administration, Miss America quickly found herself fronting a legitimate nonprofit corporation, complete with a board of directors and an executive board, and with written expectations for contestant conduct both during and outside of the competition—for example, the dictate that no young woman aspiring to or wearing the crown may ever have been married or divorced. The leadership also broadened the reach of the competition by getting Miss America into the newsreels; an estimated 112 million viewers saw Marilyn Meseke become Miss America 1938. The pageant had paid off the last of its debts by 1936, and the prizes awarded to the new Miss America, which previously were mostly of the screen-test-and-trophy variety, became more lucrative. Miss America 1939, Patricia Donnelly, received a $2,000 endorsement deal with a hat company—a far cry from Norma Smallwood's reported $100,000 in the pageant's early years, but a sign that the burgeoning institution was beginning to gain traction as a viable option for corporate sponsors. Slaughter's first effort to fund the scholarship prize, for example, can only be described as herculean in nature. Once it proved successful, however, she had more potential sponsors than she knew how to accommodate.

History has been kind to Lenora Slaughter, who presumably did some serious arm-twisting in order to thrust the pageant toward both legitimacy and financial stability. Hindsight, however, does reveal that she made at least one serious sacrifice at the altar of respectability. At some point in those early years, she reportedly inserted what is now known simply as "rule seven" into the pageant's contestant contract, affirming that each young woman "must be of good health and of the white race." According to the excellent 2001 PBS documentary titled simply *Miss America*, "All contestants were required to list, on their formal biological data sheet, how far back they could trace their ancestry. In the pageant's continual crusade for respectability, ancestral connections to the Revolutionary War or perhaps the Mayflower would have been seen as a plus." Viewed in historical context, such a practice was consistent with the eugenics movement of the era. The pageant's 1940 abandonment of the genealogy requirements, too, coincides with the beginning of the end for all but the most hard-core eugenicists—who rapidly lost momentum around the time the world discovered that the quest for a superior race had become Adolf Hitler's raison d'être, and joined the war to stop him.

Considering Slaughter's Deep South roots and the politics of the time, the systematic exclusion of minority women is not all that shocking. Viewed through a twenty-first-century lens, however, it seems remarkable that a woman with such progressive vision also saw fit to formalize blatant discrimination.

Despite this blemish, however, it's difficult to argue about most of Slaughter's initiatives and their long-term effects. By 1944—barely twenty years after the pageant's chaotic inception—the vision of a steely, big-picture woman and a thoughtful Miss America had effectively cleaned up its image. In hindsight, it's easy to point to this moment as Miss America's first significant philosophical shift, the beginning of an evolution from a mere flesh parade to an entity that would provide real opportunities for young women. The cultural criticism seemed to have waned. Miss America was on solid ground.

Or so everyone thought. In 1945, Slaughter had no idea that she was about to run headlong into a brick wall—and the wall's name was Bess Myerson.

Bess Myerson probably knew she was special. In terms of sheer elegance, talent, poise, and beauty, she was the kind of girl who would stand out in any crowd. She certainly stood out among the competition for Miss America 1945; before the finals, the media had all but declared her the winner already, with one newspaper bluntly proclaiming that "the new Miss America will either be Miss New York City, Bess Myerson . . . or somebody else."

But this year's Miss America wasn't going to encounter the smooth sailing that Lenora Slaughter must have been hoping for. Just four months after the world went crazy celebrating V-E Day, with the staggering extent of Hitler's atrocities still waiting to be discovered in Germany and Poland and Austria and Russia and on and on and on, the pageant found itself with the first—and, to date, still the only—Jewish Miss America. And Bess Myerson wasn't just any Jewish girl; she was an outspoken New Yorker who grew up in the Sholem Aleichem Cooperative Houses in the Bronx.

In retrospect, this seems like the perfect storm for that historical moment. Myerson has rarely given interviews in recent years, but when she does, like in the 2001 PBS documentary *Miss America*, they carry the uncommon weightiness of an individual who understands exactly her place in the cultural landscape: "The first night I compete with a group of girls on talent, I won. Headline says, 'Jewish Girl in Atlantic City Wins Talent in Miss America Pageant.' Now we've just learned all the details of six million Jews being killed, slaughtered, burned, tortured. And naturally it attracts attention, and the juxtaposition of the two things was so improbable. There were people that would come to the hotel where I was staying with my sister, and they would introduce themselves to me and say I'm Jewish, and it's just wonderful that you're in this contest. But how about when people came up to you with numbers on their arms, which they did as well, and said, you see this? You have to win. You have to show the world that we are not ugly. That we shouldn't be disposed of and so on however they worded it. I have to tell you that I felt this tremendous responsibility. I owed it to those women to give them a present, a gift."

Anyone, including Lenora Slaughter, could tell that Myerson had star quality. But she also had an identity and a stubborn streak, which resulted in at least one clash with the pageant boss. Having grown up immersed in a community of Jewish families, Jewish classmates, and Jewish friends, Myerson admits to being startled by the blatant anti-Semitism she quickly encountered during her brief tenure in the pageant world. A 1995 interview with the *Chicago Jewish News* asserts that several judges were warned by an anonymous caller "not to choose the Jew." Myerson herself recalls that Slaughter advised her to take the name Beth Merrick. She declined, of course, and now recognizes it as "the most important decision I ever made. It told me who I was, that I was first and foremost a Jew."

So the pageant had a problem. But instead of taking her usual approach—facing challenges head-on and attempting to transform them into substantive assets—Slaughter did what just about every subsequent Miss America executive has also done. She tried to sidestep the issue. It was a rare moment for her, one that found her back on her heels instead of proactively taking charge of the situation. By all accounts, she just didn't get Bess Myerson's back.

Although there may not have been any outward indicators that Lenora Slaughter was fumbling with how to handle the situation, the message apparently came through loud and clear to the pageant's sponsors. Myerson reportedly received far fewer invitations than her predecessors for public appearances from sponsors like Ford and Catalina. "Those companies didn't want a Jew representing them," she has said. Even during her appearances at veterans' hospitals, where a large portion of her audience had fought against the extermination of the Jewish race, she remembers encountering anti-Semitism.

With the benefit of history and information that Lenora Slaughter did not have, it's easy to look back and call her behavior in the Bess Myerson episode cowardly at best, bigoted at worst. But consider this: nearly seven decades later, there are still Fifth Avenue apartment buildings that New York real estate agents are quietly advised not to show to their Jewish buyers, because their purchase will never be approved by the building's board of directors. The story of Jewish culture in America in any era is a complex one, and certainly beyond the scope of this particular project. But this episode was an early and obvious example of two of the pageant's most consistent and self-destructive patterns: first, defaulting to a reactive position (rather than crafting a clear and firm identity and sticking with it), and second, sacrificing the young women it claims to celebrate in the name of the pageant's survival.

Fortunately, Myerson herself had the fortitude that the pageant lacked, and demonstrated the type of big-picture vision that allows significant human beings to hurdle over insignificant ones. After all, women had fought for the vote, flown airplanes, run the country while "the boys" were fighting for Europe's freedom. Women had already internalized that they had options besides dutifully staying home with the kids. The boldest among them, like Alice Paul, like Amelia Earhart, like Bess Myerson, followed through by leveraging their power into action.

Instead of sitting alone and frustrated in her hotel room, wishing she could have her picture taken with hope chests and helpful household appliances, Bess Myerson joined forces with the thirty-year-old Anti-Defamation League. Instead of spending time in department stores, as many of her predecessors had done, this Miss America launched a speaking tour. She determined that she would "make her reign one that would matter." When the ADL suggested she use her position to speak to students and community groups, she jumped at the chance. She toured 15 cities. Pag-

25

eant officials were not pleased, Myerson recalled. 'They accused me of making communist speeches sponsored by Jewish manufacturers.'"

Bess Myerson used her unique celebrity to push the pageant—uphill and pretty much against its will—toward a type of meaning it hadn't yet experienced and probably didn't deserve. Like Jean Bartel before her, she left a legacy when she handed over her crown. By the end of 1945, Miss America could both go to college and say something important to the world, from the perspective of a young woman whose voice would not otherwise be heard. Although Slaughter had tested the idea of framing Miss America as a serious, intelligent, independent young woman, it had been understood that things were done on her terms. Rather than let Slaughter's lack of faith in her potential dictate her narrative, Myerson was the first to take control of her own destiny. Ironically, it was this exact defiance of the pageant leadership that allowed her to make manifest the qualities that Miss America endeavored to embody.

Even today, Myerson continues to be considered an anomaly—significantly lauded, somewhat troubled, but a woman who evolved Miss America's image to one that was more complex, interesting, and relevant. But regardless of this progress, it was still going to be a tricky proposition to convince the country that the girl in the swimsuit and high heels wasn't just a pinup.

That was where Yolande Betbeze came in.

There is significant debate about the actual facts of Yolande Betbeze's story, although there's not much debate that she was the next to significantly propel the pageant forward. Betbeze, a twenty-one-year-old convent-educated native of Mobile, Alabama, has inaccurately gone down in pageant lore as the Miss America who refused to be crowned in a swimsuit. Among other challenges, this would have been a rather impractical rebellion for a not-yet Miss America. Even though pageant officials were frequently known to tell the winner in advance so that she might maintain her composure for the cameras, Betbeze would have had to digest that news, run backstage, yank off her industrial-strength bathing suit, and get herself into something more to her liking. Those who have actually encountered Yolande Betbeze in person might be inclined to take a position like "Well, if anyone could do it, it would probably be Yolande," and they would be right. In reality, though, the pageant had done away with this tradition a couple of years earlier.

By 1948, Slaughter and company had significantly cleaned up the pageant's image. In 1947, Barbara Jo Walker was the last Miss America to be crowned in a swimsuit, and that year's crop of contestants would be the last to show their midriffs for quite a while, as the pageant outlawed two-piece swimsuits altogether for the ensuing fifty years.

In 1950, the pageant announced that it would begin post-dating the winner's title; since most of the post–Labor Day winner's reign (as it was then called) fell in the next calendar year, the Miss America crowned in 1950 would officially be Miss America 1951. With Yolande Betbeze, as it happened, the pageant got itself enough Miss America to handle for two calendar years. And then some.

In reality, Betbeze didn't have to worry about being crowned in a swimsuit. But she certainly had some opinions about what else she would do in one. Shortly after her crowning, she bluntly put to rest any notion that she would swim with the tide when it came to the annual Catalina promotional tour, or any other event where she was expected to take off most of her clothes. Emphasizing that she had entered the pageant for the scholarships, not to become a pinup, Betbeze flatly declared that "she would be seen in a swimsuit only when she intended to swim and not for 'cheesecake' poses."

"Betbeze wore the fabled crown uneasily," according to a January 2006 story in *Smithsonian Magazine,* which giddily recounts her donation (to their National Museum of Natural History) of everything from her crown and scepter to fan letters and telegrams from Lenora Slaughter. "In 1969, she recalled to the *Washington Post* that she had been too much of a nonconformist to do the bidding of the pageant's sponsors. 'There was nothing but trouble from the minute that crown touched my head,' she said." Nevertheless, she is widely recognized as a lasting influence on the evolution of Miss America, especially since her actions "caused Catalina Swimwear to withdraw its sponsorship of the Miss America pageant and to create the Miss USA and Miss Universe pageants, both of which focused heavily on physical beauty and crowned their winners in swimsuits."

Betbeze went on to become an outspoken activist for women's rights and civil rights. Like Bess Myerson before her (and in a gesture that must certainly have added to Lenora Slaughter's rapidly accumulating gray hairs), she did not feel it necessary to wait until the end of her reign to begin her activism; instead, she launched "verbal attacks against the objectification of women in pageants while she wore the Miss America crown." With the simple acquisition of one coveted tiara, the convent-school girl from Mobile became a crusader.

The elimination of the swimsuit from prominence is easy to overstate, though it remains—even today—the most hotly debated element of the Miss America program. Betbeze's indirect spawning of the Miss USA/Miss Universe Pageants (and the cottage industry of similar competitions that would spring up in coming years) would have a greater long-term impact on Miss America than what she chose to wear during her reign. The Miss Universe Organization—which also comprises Miss USA and Miss Teen USA—-is currently co-owned by Donald Trump and NBC, and is Miss America's most direct competition. Aside from foisting upon an unwitting public Trump's criteria for female beauty (he once opined that it's impossible to tell if a woman is attractive unless she's wearing a swimsuit . . . or less), the establishment of Miss USA and Miss Universe has complicated Miss America's journey. Sure, there is general public confusion about the differences between the programs, which is difficult to correct. But the Miss USA/ Universe staff has a simple goal—find the hottest girl in the room and put a crown on her head—and they market that goal very effectively. Miss America has a more complex message, especially today, and it is sold poorly.

Yolande Betbeze wanted to emphasize talent, intellect, class, and social awareness ahead of her (remarkable) physical beauty. What she actually ended up doing was contributing significantly to a much larger debate about the traits we value and prioritize in the American woman, one that to this day Miss America's messengers have only fleetingly been able to influence. Miss America's identity has always been riddled with contradictions and anomalies. By pushing the pageant to be more progressive and substantive than its caretakers aspired for it to be, women like Bartel, Myerson, Betbeze, and even Slaughter introduced a much more demanding mission for the institution they were shaping.

In the proper historical context, though, both Myerson's and Betbeze's actions seem less rebellious than they do reflective of what was happening among women in America. Between the First World War and the end of the Second, society's norms regarding the feminine ideal had substantially shifted. Two consecutive generations of young men had left their sisters, mothers, and wives behind to fight on foreign soil, and the Great Depression had almost all Americans scrambling to exploit every resource and survival skill. Beyond that, women started to figure out that in the midst of life-and-death moments, traditional social norms about femininity could be more easily broken down. The flapper is an obvious outcome of this type of dissolution; so, too, is Prohibition and the influence of the Women's Christian Temperance Union.

In the late 1920s, talkies invaded Hollywood and threatened the career of Greta Garbo, who was told her accent was too heavy to survive the transition. Shortly thereafter, she wielded her increased power to wrestle Louis B. Mayer into submission and become the highest-paid actor in Hollywood. Is it so surprising, then, that another bright, aggressive twentysomething with a nontraditional background would follow suit and want to call her own shots? In the 1950s, Marilyn Monroe decided she was tired of being primarily a sex symbol and began a much-publicized immersion into Method Acting, alongside "serious actors" like James Dean and Marlon Brando. Why, then, does Yolande Betbeze—who rose to fame largely due to her physical and facial beauty but considered herself an opera singer first and foremost—shock so many onlookers when she decides to carve out her own path?

Incidentally, there is little evidence to support—and plenty of oral history to contradict—the hypothesis that Lenora Slaughter was opposed to the initiatives of Myerson, Betbeze, and others who pushed Miss America forward. In 1987, when Bess Myerson's life had taken a difficult turn, Slaughter shot some choice words across the bow: "It's a tragedy, but a woman in love will do stupid things." Myerson responded that she "was always impressed by her ability to sell. Those she couldn't convince, she charmed; those she couldn't charm, she simply outlasted. I watched her feed her 'dreams and ideals' pitch to hundreds and hundreds of people, and make them believe it as I believed it." And though Betbeze often seemed to be in conflict with Slaughter, plenty have speculated that the boss wanted to downplay the swimsuits, too—in fact, she battered the rebellious media into submission with her decision to crown Bebe Shopp, Miss America 1948, in an evening gown. But regarding the pageant's yearlong image, it would have been impossible for her to orchestrate alone. She needed someone like Yolande Betbeze to come along and put her foot down. When Slaughter died at the age of ninety-four, Betbeze said that "Lenora was a strong lady with a vision. The pageant simply would not exist today if it wasn't for Lenora."

Over the course of its history, the pageant's leaders have often been somewhat behind the times. Much of that is because they have expected the gratitude, humility, and inexperience of each young winner to supersede her business sense. The leadership has repeatedly learned that this is a fallible strategy, starting way back with Norma Smallwood and her insistence on being paid to crown her successor, and Jean Bartel with her progressive ideas about college-educated women, all the way through Evelyn Ay, who knew that her skills as a speaker would carry her further than her appearance alone. In this first era of the pageant, those winners who recognized and moved in step with the current cultural moment are the ones whose names seem to be remembered most often.

By 1954, the Miss America Pageant was as organized as it had ever been. Although the businessmen of Atlantic City definitely didn't know what they were getting themselves into when they decided to turn a young woman into American royalty, transformational winners pushed the pageant closer to their own ideas about femininity and the aspirations of women. Venus Ramey (1944) would eventually run for president of the United States—to say nothing of the fact that at age eighty-two, she enjoyed a brief return to celebrity after blithely shooting out the tires of a trespasser trying to burglarize her Kentucky barn. Evelyn Ay (1954), the last Miss America of the pageant's first era, was such an accomplished and natural speaker that she legendarily "outtalked Billy Graham."

The Miss Americas of the 1920s through 1954 were certainly not a monolithic entity; their contributions and influence on the pageant's identity varied widely. To answer a common criticism about Miss Americas: the compliant winners—those who contentedly smiled, waved, kissed babies, and posed with refrigerators—probably outnumbered those who pushed the envelope. But as a whole, they helped to build the first lasting nonprofit that allowed women to trade on their talent, ambition, looks, brains, and charisma in order to get themselves to college and become voices in the public discourse. For the most part, this occurred in relative privacy; although Miss America was famous, she would still generally go unrecognized by name or face in most corner drugstores.

In September 1954, the crowning of Lee Meriwether would introduce a whole new ball game.

THREE

*I*f there were some kind of pageant for the questions people ask me most frequently, the runaway winner would certainly be a version of "how was that year, anyway?" As if it's one standard experience or there's a neat way to sum things up in a couple of sentences. It's a year of your life; it's a jumble of everything a person lives through in a year, but in public and with (usually) much higher stakes. It's not like you can just say "it was amazing," because there are definitely times that it sucks. On the other hand, saying "it sucked" not only won't win you many adoring fans, but is equally inaccurate.

And after months or years or whatever of working toward the goal, you become acutely aware that it's a grown-up job you've just tap-danced and talked and strutted and willed your way into. You kind of expect that it'll be like Cinderella's Ball, and for a while it is—but then it's more like the love child of Cinderella's Ball and that movie Groundhog Day. When you put on the pretty dress every day, it feels a lot less glamorous after a while. Particularly when the carriage turns back into a pumpkin every night, and you have to shove all your belongings into suitcases again to go to the *next place. And get dressed up and smile again, as if it's the first time. Et cetera.*

The things that seem the coolest at the beginning of the year—gorgeous hotels, great clothes, gifts—are precisely the things whose allure wears off first (except flying first-class, which seriously never gets old). Don't get me wrong, I like a beautiful dress as much as the next girl, and if someone gives it to me for free, even better. But the more you acquire, the more you have to pack every thirty-six hours. Of course, you can ship it to your family's house (after all, you've probably given up your own apartment for the year), but here's hoping they have a place to put it. Because it's a lot of stuff. You wind up with a t-shirt, a keychain, and maybe a hat or a pin at every event you attend. Then there are the cute little souvenirs—glass figurines, wooden replicas of the Town Hall, silver-plated paperweights, keys to the city. If you are given an award or trophy for your work, your hosts are usually generous enough to ship it for you. (Today, I have about three cabinets full of that stuff.) And framed proclamations—I swear to God, the first time I get a plaque saying it's officially Kate Shindle Day in one city or another state, signed by the mayor or the governor or whomever, I practically need to call for smelling salts. It is just that cool. And then somehow I acquire, like, thirty. And where will I put them? In the living room of my apartment, when I go back for my senior year? 'Cause that's not at all awkward if you want to have friends over . . .

I think most people like to give Miss America gifts because it means she's taking a piece of them with her when she leaves. To them, she is Americana manifested, so she collects bits of America wherever she goes. They want to feel like their story matters, that they matter, that she will remember them. And that's kind of beautiful. But it's still not a great excuse for a lot of the crap you accumulate over the course of the year. Your hosts (quite reasonably, in my opinion) don't want to spend eighty-five bucks on flowers you'll enjoy for the three hours you're actually in the room before they default to the maid or the limo driver's wife. So you get lasting souvenirs of all shapes and sizes.

And in this department—the giving and receiving of tchotchkes—the Miss America Organization has achieved an innovation. Right after the pageant you fill out a questionnaire, and one of the questions is "what do you collect?" That way, they can tip off the giver as to what Miss America would most like to receive. I decide that it would be rather impolitic to give the real answer (shot glasses), and kind of tacky to ask for something useful (nail polish remover, razor blades, cash). But I've always liked those little blown-glass fake-antique perfume bottles, so that's what I put.

Well, somewhere along the line, there's a breakdown in communication; I arrive at a hotel in Boston a couple weeks later and am greeted by a ginormous basket with probably a thousand dollars' worth of every Calvin Klein scent on the planet. CK One in lotion, perfume, body mist, you name it. CK Be. If this were to happen today, I'd probably bag it up and take it to a department store for a merchandise credit. But when you're twenty and green and excited, all you think is "How do I do something with this before someone realizes they just spent way too much money on me?!" Answer: ship it home.

I'm still using it, by the way. I've had it for well over a decade. So, yes, Boston, thanks, I remember you, on many occasions when my skin needs a little hydrating.

I have trophies from all the pageants I ever won anything in (total: four). Talent awards, a single shining (shocking) swimsuit award, the winner's trophy. My entire competition wardrobe and three crowns—Miss Lake-Cook, Miss Illinois, Miss America. File cabinets and suitcases stuffed with videos, boxes of photos, press clippings, a few stacks of eight-by-ten photos that will probably never need to be signed for anyone. An autographed football from Gale Sayers, and one from Mike Ditka. A Tampa Bay Buccaneers jersey that says "Miss America" on the back. Vintage salt and pepper shak-

ers *from Atlantic City, one of them shaped like the state of New Jersey and the other one like a pinup-posed Miss America.*

I have a tribal stick—sorry, that's probably not the correct way to describe it, but it's the best I can do—from a Native American group in Oklahoma. On this day in Tulsa, I stand in the middle of a circle in a hotel ballroom while they chant a prayer (if I recall correctly), and then they give the stick to me to keep. I have a gigantic painting of my own head, commissioned by a group in Atlanta and executed by a well-known local artist who does billboards. As one might expect, to say that it's best viewed from a distance is an understatement. Every couple years, I wrap it and give it to a different member of the family for Christmas—most recently, I wrapped it up for my brother and his new girlfriend. We all laugh our asses off every time, which is great—and then another 364 days go by while it just sits in a room.

Life on the road, 20,000 miles of travel each month for a year, is exhilarating and draining. Someone travels with you at all times, and you have adjoining hotel rooms. Your friends aren't allowed to crash on the couch if they're nearby. You're not alone unless you literally go into your room and shut the door. If you go out, someone is keeping tabs—I nearly give one traveling companion an aneurysm when I go running around Geneva, Switzerland after a banquet one night. I tell her that I simply needed exercise; I was fine, I was safe. She is pissed.

After a couple months in hotels, I'm way more interested in a twenty-four-hour gym and a laundry room than chocolates on my pillow at bedtime. Sure, the Intercontinental and the Waldorf Astoria are freaking awesome, but eventually I sure am happy on the rare occasions when we check into an Embassy Suites. Nobody really thinks of how Miss America is supposed to do her laundry. I'm pretty independent and find a laundromat every week or so—but a mind-boggling number of Miss Americas talk fondly about FedEx-ing their dirty laundry home for their moms to wash and send back. On a regular basis. For a year. Sure, some of them have been eighteen or nineteen and barely out of their childhood homes . . . and others have been in grad school by the time they're crowned. But for whatever reason, this has emerged as their best solution.

Here's the amazing thing: as much of a pain as all that stuff can be—the unrelenting pace and the constant travel and the Miss America office being wildly disorganized and catty and passive-aggressive—I absolutely love the hell out of the job. Not just because it's fun, although there is kind of a thrill in seeing how fast I can get a read on a city I'm only spending a day in, most of it inside. And not just because some appearances are totally awesome, like going to the Super Bowl and all the assorted events that lead up to it.

There is, quite simply, one thing that makes it just about the best job I'll ever have: I get to change the world. When you get to do that, you manage to find ways to ignore the petty annoyances. And you eventually figure out a way to get over yourself for the sake of the big picture.

I am psyched when it's over; I swap my crown for my freedom, and get to go back to my own life . . . or try to, anyway, because that turns out not to be so easy after all. But I wouldn't trade that year for anything. I'm really proud of it.

FOUR

B y all accounts (and there have been many), it's impossible to argue that the Miss America Pageant did not experience massive change when it first began airing live on television in 1954.

It was not the first time that those west of the Garden State had laid eyes on the lucky young lady during her special moment, of course; the newsreels had wide reach and significant distribution. Certainly, the pre-1950s Miss Americas had been able to secure screen tests and well-paid appearances.

But in 1954, with television marching inexorably forward as a medium for the masses, Slaughter and company decided it was time for the entire country to witness the Miss America phenomenon. After a false start in 1953, a deal was struck with ABC about two months before the September 1954 pageant.

That first television contract ran into some difficulties of its own, however. For one thing, the Miss America board of directors delayed approving the broadcast because they feared that if the local audience had the option of watching the pageant at home, ticket sales for the live show at Convention Hall would drop precipitously. For another, in the end, the deal was made not by Lenora Slaughter (although one suspects she had some input) but by Miss America president Hugh Wathen. Apparently, Slaughter's vision and leadership were sufficient for the day-to-day administration of the pageant's affairs—but when it came time for big business, the men stepped in and relegated her to the background. It's a tiny detail, to be sure, but an early indicator that the pageant leaders did not entirely buy the educated, independent female image that they were selling.

That first television contract stipulated that about 125 ABC affiliates were to broadcast the show in its "entirety"—to be completely accurate, it should be pointed out that many of those early telecasts actually began before the cameras went live at ten thirty in the evening. Numerous other affiliates joined the in-progress show at eleven, after their regularly scheduled programming but in time for the crowning of the new Miss America.

As Atlantic City held its collective breath, hoping that Convention Hall wouldn't be vacant while the show aired at home for free, households across the nation tuned in to the broadcast in unbelievable numbers. Twenty-seven million viewers watched Lee Meriwether take her walk down the runway, and the pageant scored a 39 share of the viewing audience. Once again, Atlantic City foreshadowed its future as a gambling town, and another huge roll of the dice paid off big time. The massive success of the show transformed the pageant into a major network television event for the next fifty years.

Infinitely more important than any of the ratings numbers, however, were the two biggest and most lasting results of the 1954 competition—the national and remarkably indelible branding of Miss America's image, and the concept of turning an ordinary American girl into a household name overnight.

Miss America's presence on television, once and (arguably) for all, went a long way toward cementing her brand.

While the first thirty-ish years had piqued public interest, and had clearly achieved the original objective of keeping the tourists in Atlantic City for an extra week in September, 1954 was the year the pageant really exploded into a national phenomenon.

In reality, this instant brand identity has proven, over the decades, to be both a blessing and a curse. Those early, grainy images look more like a debutante parade than the actual rough-and-tumble, roll-your-stockings-down infancy of the pageant. Watching the contestants float up and down the endless Convention Hall runway in orderly formations, it's easy to understand why this soft-focus image continues to stick with the average viewer to this day. No matter what more contemporary updates have been attempted (and attempted, and attempted, and attempted), this vision of idealized 1950s Southern belle femininity has refused to budge.

As for Miss America herself? She, too, remains firmly ensconced in the minds of many as an archetype rather than an individual. Miss America is an ideal, as Bernie Wayne's famous anthem has proclaimed for decades, but in the hearts and minds of the public, she is a very specific type of ideal. She is classy, charming, charismatic, and humble. She is a lady. She has a decorous and prominent sense of purity—she may not actually be a virgin, but she sure can play one on TV. She is usually politically and personally conservative. She is both approachable and appropriate to place on a pedestal. She is pretty, but blush-of-youth pretty, and she seemingly just woke up that way one day, at around the age of sixteen, without trying too hard (see also: Lee Meriwether, 1955; Mary Ann Mobley, 1959; Judi Ford, 1969; Dorothy Benham, 1977; Shawntel Smith, 1996; Angela Perez Baraquio, 2001; Laura Kaeppaeler, 2012). Very few of those who have captured the national crown have been true bombshell-sexy young women— Yolande Betbeze (1951), Carolyn Sapp (1992), and Jennifer Berry (2007) being notable exceptions. In fact, as writer Frank Deford observed in 1971, "Most Miss Americas, when they win, are neither especially beautiful nor sexy. They become more beautiful with age."

Miss America, on balance, is usually the kind of girl a mother would want her son to marry—or as Betbeze colorfully put it, "the kind of girl who would go into a bar and order orange juice in a loud voice." If she were a car, she'd be an attractive, sensible coupe, not a pickup truck (despite her enduring heartland appeal) and *certainly not* a fast convertible with a V8 engine. For better or for worse, she is regarded by the greater public—with a fair amount of accuracy—as the ultimate girl-next-door-made-good.

And with the exception of a few specific winners—most of whom attained enduring celebrity status not as a direct result of winning the title but by virtue of the high-profile careers (and/or marriages) they leveraged it into—the institution, the image, the brand consistently remains more famous than the individual. Miss Americas have ranged in height from four feet eleven to six feet; they have possessed every hair and eye color under the rainbow (one fun game is to look back through the old Atlantic City program books at the sheer creativity the contestants employed to describe their features—not to mention their measurements). Contestants, and winners, have represented most of the prominent ethnicities in the United States, with the notable exception that there has never been a Muslim Miss America, and there has never been a winner who was openly gay—although more than one contestant has taken on gay/equal rights as her platform issue and there have been a sprinkling of out lesbian contestants at the local and state levels.

Regardless of these variations, the perceived "look" of a Miss America is remarkably stereotypical and consistent. Deford in particular analyzed the available statistics with his trademark sportswriter's precision, but in general, my experience is that the public expects Miss America to be tall (5'7"–5'11"), white—or, at the very least, the possessor of distinctly Caucasian features—blond, long-haired, light-eyed, effortlessly slender, shockingly beautiful, and tricked out in a gown and crown regardless of their appropriate-ness for any specific event. In truth, very few Miss Ameri-cas actually meet even most of these descriptors. The pag-eant itself has been significantly more diverse for many years, although it didn't really start becoming a truly inclu-sive enterprise until about 1990.

A different kind of evolution, however, unquestionably occurred in the months and years immediately following Lee Meriwether's televised crowning in 1954. For proba-bly the first time in American history, a young woman at-tained true overnight celebrity. One day she was just an-other charming, lovely California girl; within hours of her crowning, she was a nationwide household name. She was certainly preceded by plenty of female celebrities—every-one from Abigail Adams to Harriet Tubman to Clara Bow to the consortium of American women who fought to win the vote—but this celebrity status was different. It came without a climb to the top, a publicly understood back-story, or any kind of recognizable body of work. Lee Meri-wether wasn't a star. And then, instantly, by virtue of a crown, a bouquet of flowers, and a long walk down a run-way, she was.

Today, overnight fame is commonplace, although it of-ten begins with scandal. A woman selected to marry a "millionaire" on live television also becomes a household name; so, too, can a nubile, ambitious girl who gets "blind-sided" by the emergence of a sex tape (typically—and for-tunately—this kind of fame is mercifully fleeting). But the Miss America Pageant did something that very few have ever succeeded in accomplishing: it lifted a young lady out of complete obscurity without any kind of advance notice. Plenty of game-show and talent-show winners become famous these days, though usually over weeks of competition during which the field is gradually narrowed. Millions celebrate the newly minted stars of each Olympic Games, but plenty of those people watch the trials, qualifying rounds, and semifinals (and of course, there is a de facto, widely held and reinforced, and altogether correct, belief that Olympic medalists, Super Bowl champions, Academy Award winners, and the like do not just show up one day and win the biggest available prize). The country's fascination with celebrity did not begin with Miss America, to be sure, but she was a major factor in its evolution. One could even persuasively argue that the Miss America Pageant, in the mostly accidental way it did pretty much everything else, was the very earliest incarnation of the now ubiquitous reality television trend. You're not famous—and then, suddenly, you are.

It also didn't hurt that Lee Meriwether's 1954 victory by the Boardwalk launched a substantial acting career, and thereby secured her position as one of the top two or three Miss Americas who has achieved ongoing fame and recognized career success. (Meriwether, in fact, continues to perform consistently as she approaches the age of eighty.) She not only managed to acquire overnight fame, but she quickly and cannily used it as a platform to become a highly visible television and film presence. Most Miss Americas have not been able to leverage the title as successfully (although certainly not for lack of trying). It took the perfect storm of a young woman with talent, looks, charm, and a brain, a contest that earned her lightning-fast public admiration and respect, and a relatively new and hugely revolutionary type of technology to deliver her to the eager masses. Decades later, Vanessa Williams would gain far greater fame both because of and (more specifically) in spite of her Miss America win. But in those early years, the Miss Americas simply rode the instant-celebrity wave as far as it, and they, could go.

The rise of the Miss America Pageant as a television event in some ways presaged the coming cultural divide over femininity in America. Already audiences were becoming fascinated by distinctly different types of women. Traditional femininity and beauty certainly still had their place in the pantheon, represented by stars like Grace Kelly. But there were plenty of female actors who embraced more-complex definitions of womanhood. Katharine Hepburn, Greta Garbo, and Marlene Dietrich had all become wildly successful while deconstructing traditional norms of femininity. Natalie Wood's tortured-youth persona resonated with a generation. Even cinema darlings like Elizabeth Taylor (particularly in *Suddenly Last Summer* and *A Place in the Sun*) gravitated toward a darker, more conflicted identity. Finally, the rise of stars like Marilyn Monroe, Lana Turner, and the countless knockoffs who follow even now, carved out a place for women who unabashedly traded on their sex appeal. All of these elements were present in the most interesting Miss Americas, even if they were often buried under layers of white tulle.

Part of Miss America's peculiar brand of fame also represented an escape—a very public, respectable one, to be sure, but an escape nonetheless—from the average American life. Thousands upon thousands of women had embraced the "Rosie the Riveter" identity in the 1940s, only to be relegated to the kitchen again when the boys came home. Suddenly, the daily tasks that had seemed satisfying and appropriate for generations were a little less exciting—and this realization coincided with a technological moment that clearly offered some fascinating alternatives. The allure of instant fame was not new. But as embodied by Miss America, just a pretty hometown girl who suddenly seemed to have infinite opportunity ahead of her, fame ap-

44

peared far less mysterious and much more attainable. It was, in many ways, the final moment of ascent to the tipping point. Within a few short years, women would openly rebel against the mores that kept them in the kitchen; in the last-gasp-of-innocence fifties, they could at least cheer from their living rooms as the girl next door floated down a long, glossy runway of possibility.

In hindsight, it's both fascinating and frustrating to look at the pre-television Miss Americas with the knowledge of what was to come. For example, as significant as Bess Myerson's year was—and as consistently as she stayed in the public eye for decades—it's hard not to speculate about how the power of national television could have compounded her impact. What if the coronation of the first Jewish Miss America had gone out to 27 million viewers simply because she'd been born ten years later? What would it have meant for the Miss America Pageant to choose her after Hitler's incomprehensible atrocities had been fully uncovered? But, on the flip side, would she then have been embraced by the sponsors who tossed her aside in 1945? Might her acceptance by those sponsors have meant she would have been unavailable to do the more important work to which she dedicated herself during her time as Miss America? Maybe stardom wasn't what Myerson needed. Maybe she needed to be marginalized, in order to fight back on behalf of her devastated community. Maybe her impact would have been reduced by a decade's delay.

In 1921, Miss America was born. In 1954, she quickly became a nationally recognized commodity. How the pageant brass dealt with that enormous success—and how, to this day, they continue to try to harness and direct the potential of Miss America's identity—would illuminate both the definition of American femininity and the opportunities and limitations of overnight fame.

It begins: in 1921, Margaret Gorman of Washington, DC (third from right), was named the first Miss America. The Vicki Gold Levi Collection.

King Neptune, here with Margaret Gorman, presided over the festivities and was a ubiquitous presence in the early years; posing with each Miss America was one of the perks of the gig. Courtesy of Robert Ruffolo/Princeton Antiques Bookshop.

In 1922, Gorman was succeeded by Philadelphia's Mary Katherine Campbell, rocking a fur coat and closed-toe pumps with her swimsuit. Campbell also took the title in 1923, prompting a rule change that limited winners to a single victory. Still, her return to compete again cements her as the manifestation of my recurring stress dreams. Courtesy of Robert Ruffolo/Princeton Antiques Bookshop.

The Miss America parade, shown here in 1924, brought enormous crowds to the boardwalk. Atlantic City was already a popular destination, but Miss America quickly became a huge draw for the seaside resort. Courtesy of Robert Ruffolo/Princeton Antiques Bookshop.

As the annual event grew, the winner's prizes also got cooler. The now-priceless trophies—like the giant seashell given to Ruth Malcomson in 1924—were typically oceanic in theme. The Vicki Gold Levi Collection.

When Lenora Slaughter made the trek from Florida in 1935 to revive the pageant, she was only 24, not much older than the contestants she supervised. Her tenure transformed the pageant into a respectable enterprise. She is shown here in the 1950s. Press of Atlantic City.

Bess Myerson, still the only Jewish Miss America, was escorted down the boardwalk in 1946 by American G.I.'s. Courtesy of Robert Ruffolo/Princeton Antiques Bookshop.

Yolande Betbeze, shortly after her 1950 crowning—and probably not long before she flatly refused to wear outfits like this on a regular basis. Courtesy of Daryl Schabinger.

*An indelible and enduring image: debutantes floating
down the runway in miles of white tulle. The Vicki
Gold Levi Collection/Photograph by Al Gold.*

Sponsors like Philco took advantage of the pageant's popularity to create buzz for their products. Lee Meriwether, presumably, got a free TV. Courtesy of Robert Ruffolo/Princeton Antiques Bookshop.

Bert Parks (here, with Bess Myerson several years after her reign) was a recognizable personality even before he became the pageant's longtime host—but Miss America cemented his household-name status. The Vicki Gold Levi Collection.

Upon her retirement in 1967, Lenora Slaughter (pictured here with, left to right, successor Albert Marks, vice president Adrian Philips, and president John C. Rowe) was presented with a symbolic Miss America crown. Press of Atlantic City.

*Vanessa Williams, a radiant and historic Miss America,
could hardly have anticipated the unprecedented challenges
she would face. She is pictured at a 1984 press conference
at the Golden Nugget.* Press of Atlantic City.

In 1987, Kaye Lani Rae Rafko quickly made it clear that her reign would be dedicated to the unique power and importance of the nursing profession. Courtesy of Kaye Lani Rae Rafko-Wilson.

Part Two

WOMEN ON TOP

FIVE

I find out pretty quickly that not only am I kind of famous, but also that I'm completely unprepared to be famous.

The best way I can describe this disorienting experience, in general, is to say that it's both the best and the worst year of my life. Most Miss Americas—me included—come from relatively sheltered backgrounds, and we sort of wander away from our cozy college campuses as we win our local and state pageants. But there's no way anyone can prepare you for what it's actually like when you win the big kahuna. As a result, you do spend a fair amount of time trying to figure out how the hell you just become not only a quasi celebrity (which you've been super excited about being for quite a long time) but also a grown-up (which you really haven't seen coming). You are, suddenly and constantly, accountable for—and judged on the basis of—your statements, outfits, hairstyle, opinions, political positions, family religion, body type, and so on for the first time in your life. No more rolling out of bed and going to class in your sweatpants. No more off-color jokes in mixed company. No more being safely tucked away while you figure out who you are and what you value—which, no matter what anyone tells you, you do not already have all figured out by the time you win the crown.

It's like being pushed out of the nest with a red-hot pitchfork; you'd better learn to fly pretty damn fast or you're dead.

Wherever you go, you are never just yourself. You are Miss America. *And part of the reason people love having Miss America come to town is because, well, they get to say they hung out with Miss America. If they remember your actual name after a few months, count yourself lucky. If they spell and pronounce it correctly, you should give them a big fat kiss, because there's no telling when that'll happen again. And if they ever meet another Miss America, at some point in their lives, they will probably tell her, "You're my second Miss America," and then wait with bated breath to be politely asked who the first one was, because they're very, very proud of it. Which, again, is charming—the first fifteen times it happens.*

Well-meaning people, dazzled more by your position than by you as an individual (because most of this stuff gets thought up way before they ever actually meet you) often guess wrong about what you might find fun or amusing. I get into the habit of politely declining the optional "extras"— dinner at someone's house, a ride in their boat, a special tour—once I realize that no matter what anyone says about giving me a chance to relax, bringing along the Miss America persona is mandatory. It's way more fun to hang out, work out, and spend a couple hours watching TV than to go to a lovely-sounding brunch on my one day off a month (if I'm lucky) and discover upon arrival that it's a host, hostess, and thirty of their closest friends. And the jokes—THE JOKES. My favorite joke occurs about two-thirds of the way through my year, when I'm already pretty fried. I like being self-sufficient; I've always been about 75 percent tomboy, and it's weird to me that people suddenly believe that, for some reason, I can't or shouldn't do menial things for myself. So I end up basically racing whoever it is—driver, skycap, helpful volunteer—to the baggage carousel, so as to pull my seventy-plus-pound suitcases off for myself. Stupid, but it seems like a good idea at the time. A small act of defiance against the porcelain princess image, because I've never fit that image and am not planning to start.

So one day, one of the guys from the group greeting us at the airport grabs one of my suitcases and acts like it's extra heavy. And then kind of laughs and goes, "Is this the one with all the makeup?" And he doesn't mean a damn bit of harm by it. He's probably nervous, because he isn't here to meet me, he's here to meet Miss America. So he makes a dumb joke, and I immediately get all uppity, like "actually, that's the one with all my files on AIDS research." And then he feels terrible. And then I feel terrible, because seriously, no need to be a complete bitch to this harmless guy.

Except that I don't think the stereotypes are harmless, because I live with them every day. Every time I show up somewhere and someone makes a crack about how surprised they are that I'm not wearing a gown. Yeah, dude. To a grade-school assembly? Seriously? Or the time I'm invited, and then uninvited, to speak at Stanford, because somebody gets the bug that Miss America won't be able to relate to the students there. And by "bug," I mean "suggestion from a women's studies class." Which I've also taken, by the way, at Northwestern. I think I can hang, guys.

I've learned that the stereotypes, even this many years later, are an automatic companion to being a Miss America. And really, most people don't intend to be rude. I mean, sure, there are some jackasses who intentionally want to make you feel powerless, and some who legitimately believe that they can make jokes over your head without you figuring it out, because they don't expect you to be very bright (hello, stereotype . . . sit down and make yourself at home!). But for a much greater percentage of the people you meet, it's a more simple give-and-take. Like, "you were handed this great position, based partially on your performance in a swimsuit competition—so you must understand that America will naturally assume you're a bimbo, right?"

Well, no, actually not right. Here's how it actually happens: I work my balls off to become what I believe a young woman should aspire to be. I develop my talent, my brain, my physical fitness, my ability to speak intelligently in public on just about any topic you can throw at me; I focus on my adeptness at becoming, overnight, the public face of a multimillion-dollar corporation. I've given speeches to people in the upper echelons of education, world health, nonprofit work, the media, the entertainment industry, and the legislature of our country—and not only have they listened, but they've given me awards for the things that I say and stand for. I've gotten a standing ovation at the World AIDS Conference just for talking passionately about HIV education, and another from a skeptical DC insider crowd when I read my needle-exchange-related open letter to President Clinton during my two minutes at the podium.

I have come here, to your town, not just because you invited me and paid for my flight, but also to tell your students and your news anchors and anyone else who will listen all about this thing called AIDS, which will kill them if given the chance. I've researched and touched this epidemic in ways you will never bother to do, not only to help you, not only to build a fortress of credibility that gets me through this very moment almost every day, but because I believe that individuals who are placed in positions of substantial influence have an obligation to do something more than talk about their effing outfits for 365 days. I say all this not to brag, but to express to you in the most solemn fashion I can muster that if I have done all this before the age at which I can legally buy alcohol, your decision to pass judgment on my character—cloaked in humor as you may think it is—is completely out of bounds.

But, of course, I will never actually say this. Because that would be rude. And you don't become Miss America without internalizing at least some of the rules of the road. For example, that Miss America is—duh—not rude.

In the end, I don't blame those people very much at all. I actually place the responsibility squarely where I think it belongs—on the Miss America Organization's continued failure to re-brand its own product responsibly and consistently. Why, for example, does anyone still believe that Miss America is some kind of arm candy, ten years into the pageant's singular focus on the platform issue? Why haven't they crafted more effective messaging, or, at the very least, hired someone with that ability? I don't need to be "FAMOUS, famous"; I'm way more comfortable giving HIV talks at high school assemblies than working a red carpet at a movie premiere. I hold court at summits and conferences far more effectively than I do—still, to this day, in fact—at a nightclub or a photo shoot. And I also find it hard to argue that this kind of work isn't just a better use of everyone's time. But you know what they say about a tree falling in the forest, if no one's around to hear it.

No wonder Bess Myerson went off the deep end.

SIX

Once television changed Miss America (and Miss America, in a relative sense, changed television), the pageant had few options but to try to move forward. Certainly, there was a new level of interest from both the public and the advertisers; for the first time, Miss America herself became as famous as the institution she represented.

As more Americans acquired TVs, more Americans tuned in to the pageant each September. In 1958, the telecast had moved from ABC to CBS and was expanded by thirty minutes. An astonishing audience of sixty million watched the crowning of Miss America 1959, which worked out to two-thirds of the possible audience. By 1970, the audience grew to an estimated eighty million households, though the nationwide popularity of Miss America viewing parties at the time could actually translate into a figure closer to one hundred million. Regardless, the 1970 Miss America Pageant topped its own record of frequently being the most-watched show of the year by becoming the fifth most-watched show in all of television history. As Frank Deford noted, "Year in and year out there are only two things in all of the United States that have evidenced the sustained popularity to compete with *Miss America*. One is the Academy Awards; the other is Bob Hope. Were Bob Hope to crown Miss America at halftime of the Super Bowl, the nation would crunch to a complete halt, since the figures prove conclusively that every man, woman, and child in the United States of America would be watching television at that moment."

The Miss America telecast in those early years was such a smashing success that it became appointment television for families across the country. It was wholesome enough to be the one program per year that little girls were allowed to stay up late for, but also—even if it was not actually the least bit risqué—provided enough eye candy for the man of the house to shrug his shoulders and watch from his recliner.

For several years, it seemed to be enough for a contestant to simply show up, win the crown, and ride the resulting momentum until she relinquished the title to the next winner. Miss America was Miss America was Miss America. She became famous because the pageant told us she was the most deserving; she remained a draw in communities across the country because she was famous. It was a brilliantly simple equation, to the point that it was an essentially straight line to the subsequent deterioration of Miss America's identity. Her celebrity was not carefully plotted in the conference rooms of high-ranking executives. It was, more or less, an accident of sudden and widespread exposure. This, presumably, was awesome at the time. But lacking a strategy to move ahead—or any recognition of how rapidly America would evolve over the coming decades—the pageant was inevitably going to get stuck. Stuck with a self-created fame that—lacking a more significant message than "She's the one!"—would eventually become less and less interesting to the public.

It was this very success that would eventually paralyze the pageant, a phenomenon that continues even now. Decades later, facing ratings challenges that simply would not be conquered, Miss America would swing wildly back and forth between trying to copy the trends of the moment and trying to recapture the innocence of the pageant's younger days. To do that, of course, was and is a fool's errand; it's impossible to replicate the pageants of those early years. Among Miss America's biggest leadership issues (in the absence of a nation-sized time machine) is the apparent crisis over whether to turn the clock back or forward. Sadly, since the leadership can't ever quite seem to decide which path will be more effective (and don't seem to have the patience to actually sit down, craft a new corporate identity, and give it a few years to develop), the telecast tends to jerk erratically back and forth. Classic Miss America. Glamorous Miss America. Hip Miss America. Innocent Miss America. Bombshell Miss America. Perhaps that's a product of the ground the American female identity has covered since 1955; while the aforementioned Grace Kelly, Marilyn Monroe, and Katharine Hepburn (for starters) successfully negotiated bombshell innocence, hipness, and old-school classic glamour, most women define themselves within a narrower identity. Once the pageant's television infancy set up Miss America as someone who could be all things to all people, it was inevitable that the world would reach a moment when this became difficult to sustain. As Americans recognized that they had more and more choices, the goal of satisfying everyone (or even a significant percentage of everyone) became increasingly impossible. Incidentally, never have the pageant's identity problems been more significant than in the age of the Internet, which has of course coincided with the biggest and perhaps most irreparable crash in Miss America's image and marketability.

But in those early days, well, they didn't need to sweat the details.

In 1955, the year after the telecast first aired, the pageant also brought on someone who eventually became more famous than the winner herself: a jack-of-all-trades emcee named Bert Parks. Parks was an established entertainer in his own right, having enjoyed significant success on television. But this gig was to become his most recognizable role. For starters, he was a terrific showman and improviser. He effectively became the wingman to Miss America each year, guiding her toward her crown and then sending her out to greet the world. He possessed a rare gift for effectively holding together a three-hour show year after year. As many have pointed out, he was its star for all but the last five minutes, but he managed to direct the spotlight toward the contestants with delicacy, attention, humor, and grace. And he was, for decades, the pageant's most enduring constant, with the ability to put the contestants at ease and provide opportunities for their real personalities to permeate the perfect facades.

Over the years, plenty of men involved with the pageant in some capacity or other have been called (or enjoyed calling themselves) "Mr. Miss America." Of all of them, though, the most persuasive case can be made for Parks. His stamp on the pageant was indelible; he became synonymous with its identity. He was a true song-and-dance man, but also a witty and charming host. In contrast to later years, when gimmicks and reality TV "twists" frequently left the contestants high and dry—or worse, made them the butt of the joke—Parks treated them with tremendous respect. When they surprised or charmed him and the viewing audience, he enthusiastically laughed *with* them, but was not prone to laughing *at* them. And his most lasting legacy, of course, was his annual performance of the pageant's signature anthem "There She Is, Miss America" as the brand-new winner glided tearily down the Convention Hall runway. In the years since Parks's tenure ended in 1980, the song has been performed by everyone from Regis and Kathie Lee to Tony Danza to Gary Collins to Clay Aiken to, one year, the outgoing Miss America herself. No matter how many have tried it, though, the pageant's most devoted fans always seem to be far more satisfied when a host introduces Parks's original recording. It's not just the voice, of course; it's that he is emblematic of the pageant's most wildly successful era—an ephemeral moment in which pretty much everyone agreed who Miss America was, and thought that the whole enterprise was pretty cool.

The nostalgia for those early years, especially among longtime fans and viewers, is probably inevitable. It does not, however, necessarily reflect Parks's entire term as emcee. The telecasts of the 1970s, especially as the decade went on, tell the last ten years of his story—more on that later. For Miss America, as for most true, traditional American institutions, the harbingers of turmoil started to stir in the early 1960s.

Today's global culture is so interconnected through technology and twenty-four-hour news that it often seems as if we face more challenges than ever before in the world's history. In reality, it's pretty likely that we just *know about* more of them. Who knows what the sixties would have looked like if its citizens had had access to today's volume of information? Even without that, though, it's almost impossible to believe that over the course of a single decade, Jack Kennedy was both elected and killed (and then followed to the grave by his brother Bobby), Martin Luther King and Malcolm X rose to prominence and were assassinated, the Black Panthers ascended, the Vietnam War sent a generation into battle, riots broke out at Stonewall, chaos overwhelmed Woodstock, and the American flag was planted on the moon.

Although Don McLean's 1971 song "American Pie" memorializes February 3, 1959—when a plane crash killed Buddy Holly, Ritchie Valens, and the Big Bopper—as "The Day the Music Died," the phrase could just as easily be applied to many of the events of the 1960s. On the thirtieth anniversary of the crash, writer Claire Suddath examined the extensive reach and resonance of that very specific piece of music, which "turned the plane crash into a metaphor for the moment when the United States lost its last shred of innocence. McLean envisioned that last Buddy Holly concert in Clear Lake, Iowa: teenagers in pink carnations and pick-up trucks, dancing and falling in love and dancing some more. The snow fell silently outside as the country teetered on the brink of the 1960s; no one in the ballroom had any idea what would happen next."

The death of American innocence in the 1960s has filled volumes of prose, reams of poetry, miles of film, and no small amount of vinyl. The chaos and rebellion that would consume the nation, as its heart was broken over and over again, clearly manifested in a multitude of ways. Unlike their parents, often referred to as "the Greatest Generation" because of their unwavering patriotism and self-sacrifice during the Second World War, this crop of young Americans was divided. Some clung to tradition, believing that the unrest was a passing fad. But many more revolted. Against a government that was sending them to die, against social mores they felt were unjust and discriminatory, against institutions that expected them to sit down, be quiet, and conform. In other words, against almost everything that Miss America represented. Miss America belonged to Camelot, and Camelot was dead.

As starry-eyed belles dreamed of the crown, fire hoses and police dogs were turned loose on civil rights protesters. Miss Alabama hopefuls in white ball gowns glided across the stages of their state while Rosa Parks marched from Selma to Montgomery. The best and brightest of Illinois focused on the Convention Hall runway, while protesters rioted at the 1968 Chicago Democratic Convention. Sure, the pageant still aired in millions of homes, and ratings continued to rise; undoubtedly, it served as a security blanket for those we were hoping against hope that everybody would just calm down. But hindsight illuminates precisely how Miss America, as an institution, quickly began to seem remarkably tone deaf.

And of course, there was one more big headache for the pageant during this unstable time: emerging from the chaos were women named Friedan and Steinem and Morgan, the second wave of feminism, the National Organization for Women, and a mutiny against existing gender roles. This new type of feminist ferociously rejected the emphasis on physical beauty, demureness, and the traditional concept of a woman's "proper place." The second-wave agenda emphasized autonomy, activism, education, and intelligence. Through this lens, even the most basic, careless customs of the pageant—like routinely and universally referring to the contestants as "girls"—appeared to be not only old-fashioned but also a lightning rod for outrage. Within a few short years, the new feminism would take aim squarely at Miss America.

It came to a head in September of 1968. Credited by many as the first major American feminist protest, it remains one of the least accurately reported. Over the years, it has come to be known as a bra-burning mob extravaganza, which at least has some basis in truth. Organizer Robin Morgan, on behalf of New York Radical Women, drafted a press release proclaiming simply "NO MORE MISS AMERICA!" She invited "Women's Liberation Groups, black women, high-school and college women, women's peace groups, women's welfare and social-work groups, women's job-equality groups, pro–birth control and pro-abortion groups—women of every political persuasion" to protest "the image of Miss America, an image that oppresses women in every area in which it purports to represent us."

When Morgan and her group reached Atlantic City, they found that the crowd waiting there for them far outnumbered expectations. Although history remembers them as bra burners, there was actually no fire on the Boardwalk that night. The protest, instead, took aim at the "degrading mindless-boob-girlie symbol." Coverage of the event, staged as it was outside one of the biggest television broadcasts of the year, was significant. Most reports position it as the breakthrough moment of the women's movement, when the rising tensions coalesced, found a target, and went soaring past the tipping point into the public consciousness.

For the most part—aside from some biting words from Bert Parks—the pageant ignored the protesters, focusing instead on Miss Illinois, Judi Ford, the bubbly blonde trampolinist who won the crown that night to become Miss America 1969. It was predictable, in many ways, that the pageant's leaders would decline to engage the opposing viewpoint. Especially on their own turf. But the visual was insurmountable. A new type of woman was outside, raging against the machine; a traditional type of woman was inside, blithely competing in swimsuit, talent, and evening gown. Whether there were closet feminist sympathizers among that year's Miss America contestants or not, September 7, 1968, represented a visible split between the old and the new—one that would inexorably alter the pageant's image and reputation.

Of course, there were exceptions along the way. Colorado's Rebecca King (1974) stood out because of her law-student demeanor and lack of tears at her crowning, but also because she was a vocal supporter of the Supreme Court's *Roe v. Wade* ruling. The pageant was once again caught flat-footed by the arrival of a winner with a mind of her own; King's pre-recorded farewell speech a year later made a strong statement by essentially making no statement at all. Gone was the sweet-faced blonde with stick-straight hippie hair; she had been replaced by a glamorous woman who had clearly mastered the art of hot rollers. Becky King may have advanced the image of Miss America on the night of her crowning, and for every one of the 363-ish days that followed. In that last moment, though, she seemed to be a far more traditional Miss America than viewers probably expected.

A small moral victory in terms of the pageant's evolution can be identified just two years later. New York's Tawny Godin (1976) was similarly outspoken, and had a similarly unfussy, non-pageant look on the night she was crowned. A few months into her year, *People* called her "a lunge forward in Miss America's journey into the 20th century," noting that she had admitted to smoking pot, believed "abortion and premarital sex" were "matters of individual choice," and had "nothing against homosexuals." Godin, too, was glammed up on the same night one year later. Tellingly, though, Godin's farewell speech included gratitude that "America has accepted me and my beliefs for what I am."

But Godin's target audience—and King's, for that matter—had probably tuned out by then. Especially their peers, who were discovering other passions to pursue and fight for. At the beginning of the decade, for example, Phyllis George (1971) didn't seem to have much to say at her post-crowning press conference aside from talking about her pet crab. Although George was for years one of the most visible and recognizable Miss Americas, the year she was crowned represented the highest ratings Miss America would ever see again. After that, except for a near-rival spike in September 1977, the ratings slowly but steadily declined until the pageant was bumped from network television entirely.

Miss America's long, strange trip into the realm of cultural irrelevance is symbolic of the leadership crisis that has plagued the pageant for decades. To be fair, the leadership was in a no-win situation when it came to the women's movement. To eliminate the swimsuit competition, for example, would have been seen as kowtowing to the feminists who were attacking it; to tighten its grip on the alleged girlie show was perceived as burying Miss America's head in the sand. By the 1990s, the platform issue would be added to the list of requirements, mandating that each contestant choose, develop, and advocate for a community service initiative. Long after the actual seismic shift in America's priorities, the pageant recognized that the country had evolved past it. More and more, winning a crown didn't automatically make one a person to emulate, and Miss America's eventual realization of that would be a rare moment of big-picture clarity. For a time, instead of performing her talent and appearing in department stores, Miss America would spend the bulk of her year engaging in social advocacy and community activism. But by then, much of the country had moved on; she was about twenty years too late for the party.

It's certainly far from an original idea that the six ties and seventies were about bucking the establishment. Mom's apple pie was pushed aside for LSD, baseball was less exciting than Woodstock, and although Bert Parks continued to sing it to the masses each September, Miss America was no longer "your ideal" in the eyes of many of her peers. Had there been another Bess Myerson at that moment, perhaps a minority winner, marginalized by the mainstream and thus motivated to say something substantive that connected her to the counterculture, it might have temporarily stemmed the tide. But here again, the pageant's lack of organizational strategy became a liability. Miss America has always depended heavily on the massive network of volunteers who run the local and state competitions, and they have historically (although not completely) remained rooted in traditional values. The pageant, as an institution, simply isn't structured to adapt quickly to changing times, or to risk taking on a controversial identity. If it loses the support of its volunteer network, many of whom donate thousands of dollars and hundreds of hours each year to support the national organization, the whole thing collapses like a house of cards.

As the country put the sixties and seventies in the rearview mirror, Reagan-era optimism and "greed is good" capitalism seemed to open a window of opportunity for the pageant to get back on track. The intersection of glamorous excess and conservative values was, after all, pretty much Miss America's wheelhouse. Away went the simple A-line evening gowns of the seventies, relegated to the closet next to the crinolines of the fifties. Out came the shoulder pads, hot rollers, and millions upon millions of sequins and beads.

Ultimately, the pageant didn't have to decide which path to take in the 1980s. Its path was chosen for it by exactly two women. The first, a strikingly beautiful, articulate New Yorker, inadvertently turned Miss America upside down. And four years later, a belly-dancing hospice nurse from Michigan turned it right side up again.

SEVEN

To a little girl growing up in South Jersey in the eighties, Miss America holds no controversy. She is mesmerizing, beautiful, and possesses an indescribable something that I will eventually learn to call poise.

My family moves to Brigantine when I'm three. To this day, it remains a quiet, civilized little gem of an island, even as its better-known neighbors in Seaside Heights and Wildwood roll their eyes at how the media portrays their communities. It's the kind of oasis where neighbors warn each other about getting a speeding ticket for being three or four miles an hour over the strictly enforced speed limit. There are multimillion-dollar waterfront summer homes; there are modest bungalows built decades ago and occupied year-round. But one measure of its uniqueness is the manner in which the haves and the have-nots coexist with remarkable civility, equity, and respect.

Much of the small-town allure in the midst of Jersey Shore chaos derives from the fact that Brigantine is not on the way to any other part of the shore; you don't go there unless it's your final destination. It's less than ten square miles, completely bordered by ocean on one side and bay on the other. Beyond the bay sits a wildlife preserve. Unless you have a *has to find another outlet for her considerable energy. And that's how I start on the road toward Miss America.*

I have a few vivid memories of my early childhood. Skinning my knee in the driveway in Toledo, and getting an orange and a lemon painted onto the cut with iodine. Taking a test to get into kindergarten a year early, after my parents discover that I've apparently already taught myself to read by the time I'm three or four. I remember the test seeming, well, elementary; of course I know if the ball is next to the table, on the table, or under the table. Afterward, the principal wants me to sit down and read to him, but he doesn't have any children's books—so my mom suggests he give me the newspaper and let me read him the headlines. I remember falling off the jungle gym at school and then sitting in the nurse's office. The jagged scar is still on my knee to this day, but my biggest concern is whether I will get in trouble because the blood has stained my white knee socks; I do not, in fact, get in trouble for this. I remember thinking that it's a good idea to tell my first-grade teacher that I've finished my math assignment, when I've actually crumpled it up out of frustration and thrown it away; I do, in fact, get in trouble for this, when Mrs. Flanagan calls my parents to report my big fat lie. This is not a great day, but it scares me straight—I officially become the least-convincing liar on earth, and then I just give it up altogether.

The other vivid memories I have are all about Miss America.

Few people outside the zone between Philadelphia and the Atlantic Ocean, as far north as Long Beach Island and south to Cape May, really understand the yearly arrival of the Miss America Pageant in Atlantic City. The rest of the country sees it as a popular television show. Where I come from, it's the Super Bowl and the Academy Awards rolled into one—but instead of watching it from afar, everyone you know is involved in making it happen. Up until 2005, the entire community mobilizes to put on the big show—volunteer-

ing, driving contestants around, going to the parade. If you know a cop, he or she is probably on some kind of Miss America detail for about two weeks every September.

Living, as we do, a stone's throw from Atlantic City, it's highly likely we will all be involved in the pageant at some point. When you combine the geography with my parents' love for traditional values, the performing arts, pulling yourself up by your bootstraps, and educational opportunities, it's a no-brainer.

My mom has always made friends quickly, and in this case, the relevant friends are just about the classiest couple in Brigantine. Marilyn and John Feehan are a little older than my parents. They live in a modest blue house, even though it's not a secret that they have money. Their five kids call them "Ma'am" and "Sir," and so does everyone else. I can't remember whether it started as a joke, or just because Sir is a taskmaster, but it sticks. I still have to force myself to actually refer to them by their real first names. Through the Feehans, my parents meet the Plums and the Brays and countless other couples who help out with the pageant. They meet the McGintys, the Steedles, the Schillings. Before long, my mom will be singing at the wedding of Saundra Usry, the daughter of Atlantic City's mayor.

Ma'am is the head of the Hostess Committee, which is still thriving all these years after being assembled by Lenora Slaughter. The hostesses chaperone the contestants to and from Convention Hall, and to their various appearances around the city. At this point, each hotel houses four contestants, as well as each girl's state traveling companion from home. The STCs are in charge of everything the contestants do at the hotel—using the gym, getting up on time, not being late for pickup. If you're a contestant, you and your STC have adjoining rooms, and your door to the hallway is double-locked at all times. You do not answer the door. Your name is not on the reservation; everything goes through the STC (when I eventually compete, my STC, Addie, always of-

fers to iron my T-shirts before I go to work out). And once the STCs get the girls downstairs in the morning, the hostesses take over. There are two hostesses assigned to every hotel, meaning that they share the responsibility for the four contestants. One of them picks us up while the other is dropping off food at the buffet table in the parking-lot-and-press-room half of Convention Hall. The hostesses run the dressing room, they call us to the stage, they supervise the rehearsal rooms we can sign up for, they deliver the bad news if we're too tired or hungry to give up our lunch hour for press interviews. They oversee "Sleepy Hollow," the little room full of cots upstairs, where we're allowed to nap for the balance of our meal breaks when we really start to drag. They keep track of every piece of clothing that goes onstage, from the outfit for your opening number to your production costumes to your evening gown, making sure that everyone wears the wardrobe that's been approved in advance by the pageant.

The Hostess Committee throws fund-raisers, its members stay in touch all year, they take occasional bus trips to see shows on Broadway. It is the perfect way for an organized, type A achiever to dedicate herself to something interesting while still having time to walk her kids to the bus stop and get dinner on the table every night.

Duh. Mom joins the Hostess Committee.

Ma'am, as the committee head, has extra responsibilities and duties. When the new Miss America is crowned, she immediately becomes a fixture by her side for the rest of the night. She guides her to the first press conference, rides with her in the golf cart to the other side of Convention Hall and walks her into the final contestant visitation, makes sure the hostesses and the STC move the new winner's things from her normal human hotel room up to the high-roller suite where she spends her first night as Miss America. She makes sure Miss America has a moment after she leaves the stage to touch up her hair and makeup before being launched into the circus that follows (the year Vanessa Williams is crowned, my mom stands guard outside that little room so that nobody bothers her until she's ready). If you look at almost any of the photos of the new Miss America in transit— from the eighties until the year when the pageant leaves Atlantic City—you will see the same slight, dark-haired woman at her side. It's one thing being crowned Miss America, but having one of our oldest family friends at arm's length to navigate what follows has value that cannot be overstated.

When he can, my dad helps out too. The Miss America universe tends to think in fairly simple terms. My father could easily be voted "least likely to be a tough guy"; one big reason he's been successful in his career is because he looks exactly like who he is: the guy you trust with your money. On the other hand, he's about six feet four, and plenty of my friends have mentioned to me that he can be intimidating. I know where that comes from. He's reserved and intelligent and takes a while to warm up. It's probably the same reason people have spent years telling me that I'm intimidating; I'm sitting on the outskirts, feeling tall and awkward, trying to figure a way into the conversation. Wishing I had my mom's knack, my brother's knack, for being the life of the party. It's just a language I don't really speak. And apparently that scares people, so my dad gets assigned to the pageant's security team. He's one of the guys who stands outside Miss America's first press conference and makes sure the credentialed media make it in and the riffraff don't—and by "riffraff," I mean the fifty, hundred, two hundred people who might have come from her home state and are falling all over themselves with disbelief and excitement. They get to see her, of course—just not right at that moment.

Dad, and eventually my brother and I, help set up Convention Hall every year before the contestants arrive. Half of the building is a massive theater the size of an airplane hangar, and the other half is basically a blank concrete room. All my life, one of the big jobs has been getting it ready for action, right down to marking off every single parking space with masking tape. When I'm about fourteen, I get a big promotion: I'm in charge of meeting the contestants' cars at the end of the Boardwalk Parade. I have to get them to move from the back of the convertibles, where they've sat and waved while moving at a snail's pace, down onto the actual car seat to be driven back to the hall. Sounds easy—until you have to do it fifty times, with women who have literally just had people screaming at them with joyful abandon for an hour and a half. I have to ask one poor bewildered girl about six times; she just can't process my request. Finally, I look her right in the eye and snap, "Sit!" like she's a dog, and she gets it. And smiles beautifully at me as she rides away.

If you spend any significant time around the pageant, the way my family and so many other families have, it gets into your blood. The excitement that starts to bubble around the second week of every August is infectious. Even after we move about an hour away, to the Philadelphia suburbs, we go back almost every year. To volunteer. To go to the finals. To get hoagies at the White House and eat them while we watch the parade, like everyone does. To soak it all up.

Eventually, my mom starts helping out at the Miss New Jersey Pageant, which is held in our neighboring town of Cherry Hill. She judges one year; another year, she's the judges' chair. She goes to judge in Arkansas. And my dad, who's slogged it out taping off parking spaces and being a bouncer for all that time, is finally recognized as the smart, financially responsible person he is. He's invited to join the board of directors—which, to pageant people, is like finding the Holy Grail and the Ark of the Covenant buried behind your house. He serves in that position for three or four years, helping to guard the pageant's finances and build up reserve funds. And then I totally shock everyone by winning a local pageant in Illinois, and he steps aside to avoid the appearance of impropriety. Little do any of us know what's going to happen in the next few months.

People who know me sometimes find it surprising that

I've done all that. It's always been hard to explain, even to myself. Ultimately, I think it was a combination of factors. I was a dreamer, a student, a drama geek. My brother's smart, but I am The Smart One. I'm athletic, but he is The Athlete. He was popular; I was awkward. I didn't know how to talk to other girls, and I definitely didn't know how to talk to boys. I developed a lacerating wit to protect my innocence and idealism once I started to learn how cruel people could be.

For me, I think Miss America became a ticket to acceptance. Not only would I prove, once and for all, that I could hang with the popular kids—I'd figured out how to leapfrog right over them. I believed that if I could accomplish this one huge thing, it would change everything. Guys I was talking to at frat parties wouldn't look over my shoulder at my roommate. The girls who were nasty to me in middle school would finally be proven wrong. My mom would stop pushing me toward being perfect, because she'd see that I had already achieved it. I would capital-M Matter, and people would capital-N Notice.

Winning Miss America gave me all of those things and more. But it's amazing how shallow the wrong priorities feel, once you've actually had your wishes fulfilled. Thank God for the platform issue, or I seriously might have lost my mind.

In the end, it's the first hazy memory that I always come back to. I'm probably four or five, by all accounts a well-behaved, pretty animated kid who hasn't learned about feeling awkward yet. My mom, the hostess, walks Miss Oklahoma down to the beach during a bit of free time. The three of us—me, my mom, and Miss Oklahoma—stand in the sand, with my brother looking adorable a few feet away. It's late afternoon or early evening; the sun has reached that golden hour. And I look up at this person—really, she's more like an exotic creature than anything—and feel like I've been touched by something special.

And I guess you could say that it sticks.

EIGHT

In terms of newsworthiness, nothing in the pageant's history has garnered as much attention as the meteoric rise and devastating fall of Miss America 1984, Vanessa Williams. In terms of timing, hers couldn't have been better . . . with one notable and far-reaching exception. Miss America needed Vanessa Williams at exactly the moment she arrived on the scene; for those playing the long game, of course, it seems that Vanessa Williams needed Miss America somewhat less.

By the late seventies, Miss America was in a rut. Gone were the days when sixty million people tuned in by rote on the second Saturday in September. The pageant still had a loyal following and—especially by today's standards—gigantic ratings. But the formula hadn't changed enough to draw the new audience necessary to sustain those huge numbers. In the eighties, television viewers caused as many headaches for the pageant as feminists did in the sixties and seventies, and for much the same reason: as the years rolled by, there were simply more choices. Women chose from a spectrum of identities; audiences chose from an ever-growing array of TV shows and networks.

Miss America, meanwhile, had made few alterations to

the time-honored telecast structure. Wardrobes and hair-styles evolved, but in general, much of the annual program remained consistent. Sure, there were efforts to update the show. One particularly cringe-worthy attempt featured former Miss Americas singing and dancing in a produc-tion number titled "Call Me 'Ms.'" The best that can be said about it is that it was a genuine but toothless shot at catch-ing up with the women's movement. Despite the best inten-tions on the part of the Miss America leadership—although it's unclear whether the goal was actually to evolve the pag-eant's image or merely to prop up the ratings—much of the country, and most of the mainstream media, had already left the event behind. Miss-America-as-relic had become the pageant's new identity in the minds of many; the fight for relevancy would define the pageant's next quarter cen-tury and beyond.

There were, of course, a couple of changes in Miss Amer-ica's landscape that can only be defined as major, and ulti-mately proved to be bold moves that largely backfired. At the beginning of the decade, the pageant decided to uncer-emoniously dump longtime emcee Bert Parks. In charac-teristic fashion, the leadership made a mess of things; a re-porter broke the news to Parks before he had received his termination letter.

Like the pageant, Parks's shtick had begun to wear thin by 1980. In addition, as he grew older and the contestants didn't, an air of condescension crept into his performance. With each dutiful cheek kiss from a pair of Miss Americas or a trio (or more) of female dancers, Parks moved further from his "cool young uncle" persona of 1954 and closer to a less appealing identity. Still, he was practiced and effec-tive. He may have been on the way to becoming a parody of himself, but at least he seemed to be in on the joke.

By that time, he was certainly the most famous individ-ual on the stage. His cohosts each year included the out-going Miss America and an assortment of former Miss

Americas: usually Phyllis George, often Lee Meriwether, and a few others. But one moment in a single telecast is emblematic of how his influence had evolved from charming upstart to monopolizing presence. The 1977–1978 show opens with Parks's talking, disembodied head floating against a backdrop of Atlantic City's skyline. Cut to the inside of Convention Hall, where the introductions start with outgoing Miss America Dorothy Benham and continue with the guest entertainers and Miss America Dancers. And finally, Parks himself, facing upstage in silhouette, turning to the audience, Norma Desmond-style, and descending a giant staircase to great applause. At the time, it was an utterly acceptable variety-show introduction for a host; again, though, it emphasizes how entirely he had evolved from facilitator to star of the Miss America Pageant.

Watching the telecasts of the mid- to late 1970s, it's obvious that the formula had gotten stale. The production numbers were too long, featuring endless variations on patriotism, and too many non-singing former Miss Americas were being asked to sing. Most desperate and borderline depressing of all was the ongoing attempt to make the telecast more current simply by using contemporary music. Once you hear Bert Parks sing "Blues in the Night," or do the Charleston to a Wings song, you can't ever un-have that experience. In these later years, the contestants seem almost an afterthought, filler between opportunities for Phyllis George to sing the Beatles or a former state winner to perform "Feelings." It's a shame, because, given its still-significant popularity, the pageant probably could have attracted the most current artists of the day to perform their *own* songs. Instead, the audience endured the cognitive dissonance of disco music played by the Glen Osser Orchestra—an accomplished group, but one that certainly didn't count any electric guitarists among its ranks. Those years did showcase some very talented contestants and produced some interesting winners, a couple of whom were outside the box and at least one (Dorothy Benham, 1977) who was such an obvious winner that the contestant next to her—still technically in contention—turned and smiled at Benham for several seconds before her name was announced. But the pageant as a whole had become a quaint tradition with an identity crisis. Juxtaposed against the backdrop of "tune in, turn on, drop out," and subsequently, second-wave feminism, those shows seem almost preposterous.

Even an annual intervention by Miss America president Al Marks met with mixed success. Over the course of several telecasts, he made brief appearances to clarify the pageant's mission. One year, he chatted with former Miss America Terry Meeuwsen (1975) about the positive career effect of having been Miss America; another time, Marks explained the scoring in the context of Miss-America-as-well-rounded-woman. A third appearance had him flatly stating that "this is not a beauty contest." But it's hard to argue that his plain, sensible speech wasn't ultimately drowned out by the overproduced shows.

In Parks's last year, clips of the contestants' private interviews were shown in split-screen during the swimsuit competition, perhaps to balance the eye candy with a little brain candy. Even in those brief moments, the top ten finalists that night touched on freedom for women, legal careers, alternatives to becoming a homemaker by default, intelligence, whether the country was ready for a female president. Aside from one unfortunate sound bite about how becoming Miss America could help with "getting out of my accounting and back into entertainment," it was painfully obvious that even the contestants themselves had evolved beyond the telecast.

So Bert Parks was out, albeit abruptly and with a distinct lack of grace on the part of the pageant leadership. Or so the story goes. Who knows if he had actually been told in advance? Parks was a savvy showman, and could have realized that playing to the public's sympathies was the most likely path to getting his job back. No less formidable a force than Johnny Carson himself headed up a "We Want Bert" reinstatement campaign, and the pageant had to hire extra staff just to handle the massive influx of mail pouring in from all over the country. But Carson or no Carson, mail or no mail, Parks wouldn't host the pageant again. In fact, he would make only a couple of cameos at future telecasts before his death in 1992; at his last, he crashed and burned while introducing the former Miss Americas, but earned a standing ovation and won the audience's hearts with one final performance of "There She Is." His successor, Ron Ely, lasted just one year before being replaced by Gary Collins (often accompanied by his wife, Miss America 1959 Mary Ann Mobley).

What all the early 1980s chaos added up to, really, was the need for a game-changing Miss America. Despite the best efforts of pageant officials, the program had usually been pushed forward by winners who, for one reason or another, broke the mold. Not only did this kind of young woman set up new expectations for the pageant, but she also had the power to captivate the media. Some winners in the 1970s and 1980s showed hints of an ability to pull this off in various ways: Susan Powell (1981) was an Oklahoma girl who spoke her mind and dazzled audiences with her personality and talent, while Elizabeth Ward (1982) had sex appeal in spades—eventually gaining notoriety for a supposed dalliance with then–Arkansas governor Bill Clinton and her decision to pose for *Playboy*. Cheryl Prewitt (1980) had a remarkable story about the healing power of faith. Becky King (1974) and Tawny Godin (1976) both had potential as well, but none of them quite broke through during her actual year as Miss America. As with Phyllis George (1974), Terry Meeuwsen (1975), and Dorothy Benham (1977), their individual stars would shine brightest after their terms as Miss America ended; those three went on to careers as a journalist/entrepreneur, a well-known Christian broadcaster, and a Broadway performer, respectively.

Author Frank Deford may have been somewhat off base with his assessment of Bert Parks's irreplaceability, but he did zero in on one important uphill battle that each Miss America faced: the homogenizing effect of the telecast itself on the contestants. "TV traps them all into the same cookie mold. Each new Miss America is seen first in a stock setting. She is seen again, as a lame duck, one year later in the exact same setting. These are her two formative appearances that establish her image, and the sum and substance of her action includes walking, smiling, being crowned, crying, thanking, and crowning. No wonder all the girls seem the same. . . . Because Miss America is required to stay out in the sticks all year, hustling shampoo and working car circuses, she has no chance to make the additional TV appearances that could restore the identity that TV stole from her in the first place." For this institution entering its seventh decade, the need to re-brand was critical. But as long as the pageant was limited to its standard structure of crowning and uncrowning its winners, it would be very hard to create a new and exciting identity. What was needed was a Miss America who could shake things up *during* her twelve-month reign.

1984 was a year of significant change around the world: Russia boycotted the Los Angeles Olympics, Indira Ghandi was assassinated and Ferdinand Marcos was protested, Hezbollah car-bombed the United States Embassy in Beirut and kidnapped CIA station chief William Francis Buckley, the UK coal miners began a yearlong strike, Apple marketed the first Macintosh personal computers, and the Space Shuttle *Challenger* launched its first (and, tragically, final) mission. And Miss America, appropriately for this context, would change more in twelve months than she had in decades. The road to this transformation began in a middle-class town in Westchester County, New York.

T he great irony, of course, is that no one—including Miss America 1984 herself—ever expected that she actually would wear the coveted crown.

Much has been made of the birth announcements sent out in the spring of 1963, when Milton and Helen Williams shared the news that they had added a baby girl to their family. Vanessa Lynne Williams was presented to the world via cards that read "Here She Is—Miss America!" (yet another of the many, many inaccurate iterations of the pageant's "There She Is" catchphrase). Her parents' choice has been called prescient, even eerie; in reality, the cards were standard fill-in-the-blank types bought at a stationery store.

In fact, it's highly unlikely that the Williams family imagined their child's future so vividly. At the time, women of color were few and far between at Miss America. Aside from Bess Myerson and Norma Smallwood, no woman of an ethnic or racial minority had ever worn the crown. Black contestants began competing at the Miss America level in 1970, but it was 1980 before Arkansas's Lencola Sullivan became the first to finish in the top five.

Vanessa Williams does not seem to have grown up with the Miss America title in her sights. Although the pageant is fond of claiming that "every little girl dreams of being Miss America," there was no way that a young African American child in the 1960s could have anticipated exactly when she and her peers might actually be allowed to enter the contest. Instead, Williams channeled her energy into the performing arts. After being voted "Best Actress" in her high school graduating class, she continued her studies in the highly regarded musical theater program at Syracuse University. While it's always been fashionable for Miss America contestants to bury their ambition by claiming that they entered the pageant on a lark—or even a dare—Williams's own account appears to verify that in at least one case, this was the reality. In the midst of her college years, she was aggressively recruited by a director from the Miss Greater Syracuse pageant. She needed scholarship money, and the show she was scheduled to perform in had been abruptly canceled. So she decided to give it a go.

In September of 1983, Vanessa Williams was not the only African American contestant at the pageant; in fact, four black women were among the state representatives. Unlike the other forty-six titleholders who arrived in Atlantic City that year, the minority women were treated by the media as almost an "other." While they were lauded for having made it onto the traditionally white playing field, they were simultaneously expected to carry the burden of American racial politics on their shoulders. The four black contestants were often asked to pose together for photos, "as well as questioned incessantly about 'what it felt like to have a chance to become the first black woman to win the crown.'" In the view of Sarah Banet-Weiser, author of *The Most Beautiful Girl in the World,* the presence of black women at Miss America served as a symbol to the media and public that diversity was "alive and well." This, of course, was both a drastic oversimplification of race in America and, for those who simply wanted things to go back to the way they used to be, a convenient exit ramp to stop thinking about race relations. Almost a quarter century later, the same could be said of the election of President Barack Obama. Americans who simply wonder "are we there yet?" might see it as its own endpoint, but a more nuanced cultural examination reveals that one black president does not right all wrongs. Neither, of course, would one black contestant at Miss America, or four . . . or one winner . . . or two winners . . . or, as of this writing, eight.

For these contestants, the pressure to perform could have been crippling, saddled as they were not only with the normal competition stress, but also with the conflicting goals of assimilating into Miss America's traditionally white culture while still serving as ambassadors for their ethnic community. Williams, however, seems to have thrived amid the complexity. On her way to winning the title, she picked up the preliminary swimsuit and talent trophies. Some would say that Vanessa Williams skated to victory. Others have suggested a variety of factors that might have contributed to her remarkable success: Was it her lack of over-rehearsal due to her brief tenure on the pageant circuit? Was it that the pageant was ready for, and in fact actively seeking, an African American winner, and she was the strongest candidate? Or was it simply that Williams knew that in order to reach the highest level of this particular institution, she would have to be better than her rivals in order to be considered an equal, and *much* better if she hoped to actually win?

To be sure, the Miss America Organization as a whole has not had the smoothest relationship with ethnic diversity. Even today, there are heated debates in online fan communities about what the "ideal" Miss America actually looks like, how big a role race plays in a winner's selection, and whether pressure exists within the upper echelon to crown ethnic women for appearance's sake.

As is true of the race debate in our nation as a whole, there is no answer that satisfies everyone. In fact, some of the pageant's own supporters and fans remain unconvinced that MAO is an ethnically inclusive enterprise—or, more disturbingly, that it should aspire to be one at all.

Miss America's own integration has not been without internal controversy. One longtime state pageant judge, off the record, describes walking out of a 1993 judges' meeting in a particularly conservative state after the executive director implied that the committee did not want the judges to select the state's first black winner, even though she was a clear favorite and, less than three months later, went on to become Miss America. For years, organizers of the Southern States' Ball, held off-site a few hours before the Miss America finals, would prompt the audience to "please rise for the singing of our National Anthem"—which was none other than a passionate rendition of "Dixie." This tradition continued as long as the pageant was held in Atlantic City; for the record, the last competition by the Boardwalk was not, say, 1974, but, in fact, September 2004. Perhaps most shocking, a state director who helped prepare perhaps the most ethnic-looking of the African American winners tells a chilling story of three southern state executive directors approaching her moments after the crowning to ask whether she was responsible for "that blue-gum n****r" winning the title.

Ironically, despite all the Miss America Organization's efforts to redefine its own image over the decades to reflect a more contemporary aesthetic and values system, it may well be said that a consortium of its own supporters continually thwart its evolution.

Initially, Vanessa Williams's victory was met with an outcry of support. Anyone with eyes and ears could recognize that she represented herself remarkably well on the telecast, demonstrating a potent blend of poise, intelligence, vocal talent, beauty, and the type of star quality that clearly set her apart from the field. The media response was tremendous, with the *New York Times* announcing in a headline "Black Leaders Praise Choice of First Black Miss America." Her style, poise, and outspokenness—on issues like reproductive rights and the Equal Rights Amendment—did not go unnoticed. The most striking juxtaposition, though, was between assimilation and diversity;

some heralded Williams's win as proof that We Are All The Same, while others were far more proprietary in their celebration. For his part, NAACP executive director Benjamin Hooks likened her to Jackie Robinson.

Although the crowning of the first African American winner was hailed in most quarters as a landmark event, the life of the actual woman who wore the crown quickly proved to be far more complicated. Simply put, there was no way an aspiring Miss America could anticipate the pressure Williams was about to face. Like all Miss Americas, she would immediately encounter the difficulty of reconciling her own identity with the decades-old image of Miss America as a whole. Like many, she would come face-to-face with the pressure of representing an organization that seeks to capture and capitalize on America's feminine identity, especially in the context of the ongoing women's movement. But she alone among Miss Americas would also need to navigate the more specific layers of racism and African American ideology in the America of the post–civil rights era.

In contrast to Bess Myerson, Vanessa Williams seems to have settled on a Miss America identity that, while inclusive of her ethnicity, was not predicated upon it. While Myerson actively rejected the insinuation that her Jewish heritage was contrary to the Miss America brand, stepping away from the traditional yearlong dog-and-pony show in order to become a social agitator, Williams represented the somewhat milder Reagan-era practice of nodding respectfully to diversity while identifying her race as merely a single aspect of her identity. "I think I would be doing the same thing if I were Spanish or white or Chinese," Williams said at the time. "I am still a person, I still feel the same way about being crowned. I don't think they chose me because I was black and it was time for a black Miss America. They chose me because they thought I could do the job."

Although she had undoubtedly digested how her racial differences were explored during the competition, her life after winning the crown showed how the very things that caused her to be celebrated also had an ugly underbelly. Her parents were deluged with congratulatory letters in the first week. But, as her mother, Helen, later recalled, they soon began to receive a different type of mail: "Someone wrote that they were going to throw acid in her face. People sent notes: 'YOU'RE DEAD, BITCH,' 'You'll Never Be Our Miss America,' 'You're all black scum.' I gasped the first time I saw some of the contents. Some letters had pubic hair in them; some had spit; some had semen. They had an agent from the FBI show me how to open mail, so, if necessary, they could take some of the letters and trace them back to where they originated. I wore gloves and opened the mail with a letter opener. I'd never take the stuff out—it was just too disgusting."

Personal appearances, especially in the South, necessitated extra security measures, including nearby sharpshooters as she rode in her hometown parade. Even when no one's life was on the line, Williams's victory was ruthlessly dissected by writers and observers of every race. Scholar and author Gerald Early, for example, ruminated about the significance of this Miss America even as he waited in line with his family to meet her at a St. Louis department store. Would a black Miss America, as he overheard some women saying, "show black men that we're as good as white women"? Was it simply very public proof that black women were also beautiful, a representation akin to the crowning of Bess Myerson? Early is alarmed by the possibility of the former, fearing that perhaps "black women needed some giant manufactured event of American popular culture to make them feel assured that they were and are, indeed, as good as white women." But one thing that largely escaped mainstream conversation was the reality that Williams happened to be a black woman with light skin, light eyes, a narrow nose, a slender figure, and straight hair. Her features, her speech, her body were far more Caucasian than ethnic . . . and for this, too, she would be criticized. "She does not look like the little black girl of the inner-city projects who reeks of cheap perfume and cigarette smoke and who sports a greasy, home-made curly perm and who has a baby at the age of fifteen for lack of anything better to do," Early continues. "Vanessa Williams will not even in a distant way remind anyone of *that* hard reality."

Unfortunately, Williams would soon face her own hard reality. In July 1984, about eight weeks before she was to crown her successor, she was informed that explicit modeling photos taken two summers earlier were going to be published by *Penthouse* magazine. Although she claimed she had never signed a release for the pictures (and eventually sued *Penthouse* publisher Bob Guccione for printing them), the news was a devastating blow to her tenure. For their part, the pageant leadership was between a rock and a hard place. Future CEO Leonard Horn—who served as the pageant's legal counsel during that time—has said privately that if Williams had not resigned, it was unlikely that her bosses could have legally fired her. However, he has also painted a vivid picture in which the *Penthouse* incident could have dragged the whole enterprise under. Recounting the incident in 2001, he claimed that the television sponsors were poised to pull their advertising from the pageant broadcast "if we didn't handle this right." Horn further asserted that "if they pulled out at the end of July, there would have been no money and no Miss America pageant in 1984. And there would not be a Miss America pageant today."

Williams resigned from her station just as she had ascended to it, amid a firestorm of media attention. First runner-up Suzette Charles (who, by also being of African American heritage, allowed the pageant to dodge a giant bullet) served just six weeks before Miss Utah, Sharlene Wells (1985), was crowned the pageant's first Mormon Miss America.

Even today, the Vanessa Williams story remains both cautionary and controversial. As Hollywood starlets continue to learn, the casual nude photo is a powerful skeleton in the closet of a young female celebrity. But Williams's legacy, bolstered by her subsequent career success, has made her both an underdog to root for and an enduring symbol of grace under extreme pressure. Interestingly, she is remembered as a favorite Miss America by pageant fans and the media alike, albeit for different reasons. Journalists and academics still debate her significance, as an example of evolving ideas about race in America (particularly gender-based norms about black women, sexuality, and the Jezebel stereotype) and as a feel-good story of a woman who triumphed over adversity to become the most famous former Miss America of all time. The pageant's faithful volunteers and fans, so disappointed by Williams's premature exit, generally speak with great reverence about her. They may be conflicted about the scandal itself, but most admire how she actually performed her duties during her ten months with the crown. In 1988, with the aftermath of Williams's resignation barely consigned to the rearview mirror, Academy Award–winning author William Goldman was invited to judge the national competition. His observations and conversations regarding Vanessa Williams indicate that many fans were still enthusiastic about counting her among the pageant's alumni: "I remember talking to some pageant people and they said that the best Miss America they ever had was Vanessa Williams. Apparently she was just sensational. She was just the most verbal, bright, terrific seller of the Miss America contest they'd ever had."

As long as the Miss America program exists, so too will the conversation about Vanessa Williams. How did the controversy truly affect her future? Was her status as the fallen Miss America ultimately the springboard for a successful career, or simply an obstacle to overcome? Did the leadership address the scandal with the same grace it expects from its young titleholders? Finally—and most frequently discussed in some circles—if a similar situation were to arise today, would the pageant's strategy differ from the one it adopted in 1984? These topics, and others, are still hotly debated. The release of Williams's 2012 memoir, *You Have No Idea*, in which she publicly discusses the subject in more depth than ever before, served as a catalyst for the reexamination of her notorious year with the crown. One issue, however, has already achieved consensus: as much as Miss America may have changed the life of Vanessa Williams, she, in turn, left an indelible mark on Miss America.

In September 1987, the annual ritual was again under way. Fifty contestants showed up in Atlantic City with the unassailable knowledge that only one of them would leave with the crown. Among them was an unassuming registered nurse who would also make her mark on Miss America, albeit in a very different way.

Kaye Lani Rae Rafko arrived on the Boardwalk—from her hometown of Monroe, Michigan, where her father owned a junkyard—with an unlikely name, an unusual talent, and a unique goal. Though her family had discouraged her from competing in pageants, she eventually did so anyway in order to earn scholarships to pay for her studies at St. Vincent's School of Nursing in Toledo, Ohio. Six years and fourteen pageants later, she had won more than $45,000 to that end. For the talent competition, she performed a dizzyingly elaborate Tahitian dance; she was crowned Miss America in a refashioned donated wedding gown. Before her Atlantic City victory, Rafko memorably— if unwittingly—was featured in Michael Moore's Rust Belt documentary *Roger and Me*; the filmmaker framed her as an out-of-touch daughter of privilege who cared more about her fortune at the national pageant than about the plight of factory workers in her home state. Moore, like almost everyone else, failed to recognize that she was a working-class girl who would not only go on to win the pageant, but would set Miss America on a trajectory toward lasting and significant social relevance.

Rafko was visibly shocked when she was announced as the new Miss America; in those days, the runners-up and the winner were still announced directly from the top ten, instead of first being whittled down to a top five. Her crowning moment began with the remaining six semi-finalists standing in a line. When her name was called, she manifested the crowning moment fantasy of just about every Miss America fan, radiant with surprise, humility, joy, tears, and sparkles. Unbeknownst to most, however, was the reality that this Miss America didn't plan on simply going along with the tide.

Shortly after her crowning, Rafko announced that she wanted to merge her year as Miss America with her life as a professional nurse. Not only did she plan to eventually open a hospice in her hometown, she also wanted to discuss the issues that she and other oncology and hematology nurses faced every day. Cancer treatments. Death. The rapidly spreading HIV/AIDS epidemic. Although other Miss Americas had recognized that the title was an avenue for social change, this one purposefully and specifically directed the white-hot spotlight toward things that Miss America was not expected to talk about.

Like just about every other substantive change to the institution, a straight-talking Miss America with a cause elicited a mixed response. Although Rafko received an impressive collection of supportive mail—by her own estimate, "thirty-five to forty letters a day"—she was also a target for public criticism. Although she was indisputably an aggressive and valuable advocate for nursing careers in the midst of a serious shortage in the field, some detractors felt that her Miss America title compromised the integrity of the medical profession.

Rafko, however, would go on to have the last laugh. Within weeks of her crowning, she "addressed a Congressional subcommittee in Washington, DC, concerning issues facing the nursing community." Eventually, she would work with organizations like the American Cancer Society, the American Heart Association, and the March of Dimes, and speak to the international medical community, from Malaysia to Paris and beyond. Her topic was consistent: not car sponsors or her workout routine or whether the crown was made of real diamonds, but nursing. Later, the American Nursing Association would praise her for her work, saying that she "single-handedly alleviated the national nursing shortage during her reign by speaking out on the need for more nurses." As her year went on, she crafted a legacy for herself that was not lost on even cynical pageant commentators. In his 1990 book *Hype and Glory*, William Goldman (a judge that year) observed her onstage moments before she crowned her successor: "Kaye Lani is a practicing nurse. But she doesn't just work for your ordinary GP. She works for the dead and dying. 'I'm going back to school in the spring, to start work toward my Master's degree in oncology, which is the study of cancer, with a minor in business administration . . . so that one day I *will* open my own hospice center for all terminally ill patients, both cancer as well as AIDS.'"

Rafko's passion for her work, however, and her eagerness to deal with even the darkest moments of life and death, was not the only significant shift that year. As fate would have it, 1988 was also the first year without CEO Al Marks, who retired after a twenty-five-year association with the pageant; he would die almost exactly two years later from complications after a heart attack.

Marks's successor, Leonard Horn, was a brash, outspoken attorney who had spent years as the pageant's legal counsel and had been the primary voice of the pageant during the Vanessa Williams incident. Now at the helm of the company, Horn decided that it was time to make some changes. Within a few years, he would replace the executive producer of the telecast, tinker with the pageant's formula, and introduce audience-driven interactive elements to the show. He would eventually tackle what he saw as an outdated image of Miss America, frequently commenting that he was tired of over-styled hair, evening gowns that aged the contestants, and a generally robotic breed of Miss America hopefuls who bore little resemblance to the young women they were supposed to represent. Horn once described the tipping point for his fervor as the moment he walked out to a hotel pool during pre-pageant festivities and saw a handful of contestants sitting around in full hair, makeup, and meticulously planned outfits; he wanted the pageant to find its way back to a youthful image. By 1994, he had even banned professional hair and makeup artists from the backstage areas in Convention Hall. Although it's a semi-open secret that this change was actually a result of soaring union costs, not pageant philosophy, Horn successfully spun it in the media as a move to embrace a more natural, self sufficient Miss America contestant.

To be sure, Horn could be a opinionated taskmaster, and his leadership and communication style alienated as many pageant supporters as it attracted. But he also started to do a lot of listening. He listened to the media, the pageant's critics, and most important—at least at that moment—he listened to Miss America. Horn quickly recognized that Rafko's nursing and hospice crusade was gaining the very type of acceptance he craved for Miss America: respect from the press, an individual identity for Rafko herself, and appearance requests that went far beyond the traditional autograph sessions and photo shoots with sponsor products. Miss America was still traveling extensively, but in

1987–1988, she was also building a body of work and gaining a new type of fame. Like Jean Bartel, Bess Myerson, and a handful of others, Rafko was becoming a transformational Miss America merely by talking about something besides what she was looking for in a man. Almost by accident, she had leapfrogged over the public's expectations for Miss America and into a whole new realm. Although there have been plenty of Miss Americas who probably had the ability to do this, 1987-88 was the perfect storm for redefining the pageant: a passionate, nontraditional winner, a higher-than-normal amount of America's attention as Vanessa Williams began to rebuild her public life, and, most critical, a leader with enough vision to latch on to a good idea when he saw one.

While Rafko was busy passing on the crown to her successor, Minnesota's Gretchen Carlson (1989), Horn was behind the scenes, cementing this Miss America's legacy. In short order, the pageant announced a new component for the following year's competition. In addition to the traditional disciplines of swimsuit, talent, evening gown, and interview, each contestant would be required to develop a community-service initiative. The platform issue, as it became known, was intended to evolve into the focal point of each young woman's year. This new program would not be limited to Miss America herself, or even to the fifty state winners; it would begin at the local level and fundamentally alter the priorities of each contestant. In addition to studying up on current events, social issues, and various other topics that might arise in the private interview, the young women would now have to become experts on the subject they selected.

The platform issue was nothing short of revolutionary, especially given the public's waning interest in the pageant. It was one thing to sell the program as a grantor of scholarship dollars, or to point out that the talent competition attracted young women who were well-rounded. Ultimately, though, those were just talking points—and boring, unsexy ones at that. With this new addition, the pageant had the potential to restore credibility among its longtime critics. Miss America would no longer simply be famous for winning a one-night competition. In the dawning era of the platform issue, she would have a mission to accomplish and a message to bring to the world. The next generation of Miss America titleholders would have the ability to "matter" in a way that had eluded their predecessors. At the close of the 1980s, it looked like the pageant had found its way back onto the path to relevance.

NINE

By 1998, one refrain is so familiar that it occasionally threatens to become tedious. When in doubt: platform, platform, platform.

By the time I take over the crown, the platform issue is an essential part of Miss America's identity. Not that I'm complaining; it is both the most interesting and the most challenging part of the gig.

My pageant career has been relatively brief: four local pageants over the course of three years, only one of which I actually won. Three months later, a trip to the state pageant in Illinois. And finally, the big kahuna: the Miss America competition in Atlantic City. I have exactly one local, one state, and one national crown; some contestants who revisit their state finals each year until they "age out" have five or six or even seven local crowns. And what do you do with them afterward? I've heard of women putting crowns on their wedding cakes, using them to hold the dip at parties, even freezing them, full of water, and dropping them into the punch bowl. That, I guess, is what you do when you have lots of local crowns. I only have one.

I say this not to brag, but because I believe that there is one simple reason why I don't win for the first two years and *then explode in the third. Simply put, it is nothing more or less than a growing, passionate, and incredibly satisfying focus on my platform issue.*

In the beginning, I don't really know what my platform should be. I've attended, and liked, Catholic high school, especially its focus on ministry and volunteerism. My faith has never been something I shout about from the rooftops; after all, we Catholics are a little more under-the-radar when it comes to spreading the Word than many of our Protestant counterparts. But since I've generally stayed out of trouble, and since I largely credit that to the lessons I learned from the priests and nuns, my first platform focuses on encouraging youth morality. It's hard not to look back and judge that, knowing, as I do, what will eventually follow. More than anything, it is well intentioned but utterly toothless and generic. I don't know the first thing about the challenges some kids face—those who barely have parents, those for whom it's much easier to give in to a life of crime than it is to make it through tenth grade, those who never get to college. I've never gone to class hungry in the morning, or gone to bed hungry at night, because I only get one meal a day, in the school cafeteria. I've never walked home worried that a hail of bullets would suddenly be launched at me from a passing car. I've never laid eyes on drugs, let alone been pressured to try them. So the truth is that my first platform is basically preposterous. Because even though I believe that good things are possible if you make the same choices I have and avoid the same risky behaviors I've avoided, I have no context in which to understand why lots of kids don't. It's a bullshit platform that sounds good at the time, chosen merely to satisfy a requirement and have something to write on the appropriate line on my pageant application.

The second year, I try a little harder. Motivating youth (or whatever version of that phrase I actually use) may have been just as sterile and undeveloped . . . but at least I can look back and say that it was less judgmental. Better, I think, to say "yes, you can!" than "no, you shouldn't!" The problem, once again, is that I really don't spend any time on it. I still don't learn much about the seedy side of teen complacency. I genuinely believe that anything is possible if you work hard for it, but I fail to factor in the reality that some kids—like me—come from circumstances that make achievement far easier (unfortunately, it's still going to be a few years before Malcolm Gladwell writes Outliers, *which could have made all this much easier).*

The platform I end up with, the one that ignites my passion, doesn't actually start out as a platform at all. It starts with a class at Northwestern. "Rhetoric of Social Movements" fulfills a credit requirement for the second major I've picked up, in sociology, and it piques my interest. The professor, Scott Deatherage, has a major résumé as a debate coach; in fact, when he dies in 2009 at age forty-seven, I will learn that he's the "winningest coach in the history of national collegiate debate." I'm not all that interested at the time in learning how to debate, but I'm fascinated to learn the ins and outs of social activism. It's a class with a lot of reading and very few tests. The big assignment—basically the make-or-break for your whole grade—is to volunteer for ten hours for any initiative you like, and then write a paper on it. When I go back to Northwestern for my post–Miss America homecoming celebration (and then later, for my senior year), I don't run across him. One of my few regrets: I'm not sure Scott Deatherage ever knows how significantly he changes my life.

It's early spring 1996, my sophomore year, when I start researching organizations that will let me volunteer for them. I don't know much about AIDS at the time, although what I do know is impactful and fairly personal. I've lived in a cocoon that's been free of the epidemic for much of my life. When I graduate from high school, I don't know one person who is even openly gay, let alone HIV-positive—at that time, the two are still so linked in the public consciousness that it seems sensible to connect them in my mind.

Showing up in an established, successful university theater department is a different story. Practically since my arrival in Evanston, the HIV/AIDS epidemic has been elbowing its way into my immediate universe. On the first day of orientation, the chair of the theater department gives a speech to the incoming freshmen. Aside from the typical welcome-to-the-neighborhood comments, and his ruminations on being an artist, Bud Beyer (who will become my acting teacher for the rest of my time here) spends a few minutes talking about the need for us to be careful and safe in the midst of getting to college and letting our hair down. I remember that he specifically says "AIDS is here." I remember not knowing exactly what that means, and also that the look on his face tells us he's not messing around.

It turns out that shortly before I've arrived, a beloved and respected dance professor has died of an AIDS-related illness. It's not the first time this theater program has lost one of its own to the disease, but it is particularly painful this time. I realize that, indeed, AIDS is here. And by "here," I don't mean "at Northwestern"—I mean "in the life of Kate Shindle, an upper-middle-class, white, Catholic, conservative teenager who's never thought she'd have to worry about HIV."

Sadly, the epidemic has been creeping into another quadrant of my life as well. Also early in my college years, my mom calls to tell me that a close family friend of ours has been diagnosed. He hasn't been identified as HIV-positive; he's skipped directly to full-blown AIDS. What really makes an impression in this situation is that no one, but no one, is talking about it. My mom tells me, and she's probably told my dad and my brother. But other than that, we're sworn to secrecy. Uncle Bob, as we call him, has already lost his father; for reasons that are all too common when it comes to

HIV, he and his mother have decided to keep the diagnosis absolutely private. For the next few years, everyone knows Uncle Bob is sick. But very few know that it's AIDS.

So when Scott Deatherage sends us out into the world to get involved in social activism, I have an idea of where to look. I research HIV/AIDS service organizations, trying to find a place that will accept a volunteer with little previous experience and no qualifications except the desire to help.

I find what I'm looking for at Test Positive Aware Network on Belmont Avenue. It's a hike from Evanston, but at least the el train stops nearby (in hindsight, I'm surprised by how much of my adult life has been shaped by accessibility to public transportation). TPAN, as it's called, holds a periodic volunteer orientation, required for everyone who wants to help out—even if you just want to stick mailing labels onto envelopes. And so, one cold and rainy Chicago night, I go to the meeting and am officially cleared as a volunteer.

Make no mistake, this is not sexy work. I'm not wearing a lab coat, designing strategies, or applying for grants. I'm answering phones in two-hour shifts, often unsure of how to connect someone to a specific extension (I take a lot of messages). I'm helping out with mailings, and collating, and filing. Eventually, I'll become part of the "buddy" program, and stop at the store for cat food on my way to hang out with Hugh, who's mostly homebound because his health is deteriorating. But somewhere amongst all of this, having completed my course requirement but with no desire to stop visiting TPAN, I discover their library.

I first peek in there hoping to find some data and statistics for my term paper. What I find in that small room stacked with books and binders will set my life on a completely new course. I pull things off the shelves and pile them onto a table; before I know it, I have more information and research than I can ever use. Lurking in the stack is Randy Shilts's book And the Band Played On. *It documents the earliest days of the AIDS movement—before anyone knew why oth-*

erwise healthy gay men were dying, and while medical professionals were struggling to figure out what was happening—and both his writing and the HBO movie it inspired stir anger in me. With the benefit of hindsight, I can see clearly what those early researchers were unable to uncover in time to stop thousands and thousands of deaths.

In 1997, as I sit in that resource center on Belmont Avenue, we know exactly what causes HIV/AIDS. Not only that, we know how the virus is transmitted, what the greatest risk factors are, and most important, precisely how to stop it from spreading.

But there's a problem, a big one, and it will fuel my engine throughout my year as Miss America and beyond. Although we can stop HIV, we aren't stopping it. Why? Because of fear. Because of politics. Because most Americans shy away from the kind of frank talk about AIDS that would save people's lives. It is almost always easier to be part of the silent majority than it is to be one of the vocal minority; in this case, it's easier for people to stay in their seats at PTA meetings and city council hearings while the passionate few are shouted down by dedicated preservers of the status quo. HIV is spreading because accurate information is simply not making its way into schools and communities around the world. Lots of people hold out hope for a cure—unlikely, of course, since eradication of a virus has always been far more attainable than medically reversing its transmission—but even I, at age nineteen, can understand that the only way to combat HIV/AIDS is to stop people from getting the virus in the first place.

But AIDS, as it turns out, is an illness that brings out the worst tendencies of human nature. Because it spreads through traditionally taboo behaviors, contracting HIV is met with judgment, suspicion, fear, anger, and general ugliness. When a family member or friend is diagnosed with cancer, the first question is usually "how can I help?" But when it's AIDS, far too many people wonder, "Well, what did he (or, increasingly common, she) do to get it?" Coupled with all the misinformation floating around—that you can get HIV by kissing, touching, drinking out of a water fountain, swimming in a pool, or going to elementary school with an HIV-positive child—this tendency toward blame, instead of compassion, will prove to be fatal for millions of people. The ugliest consequence of the spread of HIV is that public figures insinuate—or say outright—that it is a punishment from on high, handed down to rid the world of sinners (sort of the viral version of the Great Flood), and it has already created a stigma that makes people with AIDS hide. Or lie. Or pretend they aren't sick, and delay too long before they seek treatment.

These days, when I advise Miss America contestants about choosing a platform, I tell them to figure out what makes them angry—because when they can do that, they will discover their specific passion for making the world better.

The HIV/AIDS movement becomes exactly that kind of passion project for me. My volunteering experience leads me to sign up for Alternative Spring Break. Along with a bunch of other Northwestern students, I go to San Francisco and Oakland to spend the traditional vacation week doing hard labor. While our friends drink mai tais in Cancún, we clean out a garage and serve meals at a soup kitchen. While they chill out on the beach in Panama City, we build a patio and water-seal a deck at a hospice. While they take pictures of their frat brothers, we carefully hang up individual panels of the NAMES Project's AIDS Memorial Quilt so that they can be photographed. The quilt panels, which family members and friends create to commemorate those who died of AIDS-related illnesses, are beginning to deteriorate; the goal is to archive every one of them on film. While there, I meet a woman who has moved to San Francisco because every single one of her friends has died. I'm at an impressionable age anyway; suffice it to say that this makes an impression.

Ironically, once I realize that the cause I have become pas-

sionate about is far more important than winning a pageant, I begin winning pageants. My competition interviews start to focus on ending a disease, not on my fitness routine or my career plans. Almost by accident (and later, with plenty of strategic guidance from people who know their way around interview technique), I refocus my ambitions on making the whole thing bigger than myself. Pageant judges are people, after all, and when people give up their free time to pick the winner of a contest, they tend to want that young woman to make a mark on the world. Otherwise, they truly are just judging singers and dancers and swimsuits and dresses. Only by connecting the competition to an issue that transcends those individual elements—an issue to which I truly intend to devote my year—do I make it to the next level. And then the next. And then the last.

We always like to say that there's no typical day for Miss America, and in many ways, that's completely true. But when I flip through my (uncharacteristically) neatly organized schedules from the year, I see many of the same things. News show after news show. Fund-raising chicken dinner after fund-raising chicken dinner. Legislative meeting after legislative meeting; site visit after site visit. And my favorite of all: school after school after school after school, across every demographic group and age group and location. Bleachers full of hundreds, classrooms with small groups of twenty-five, many of whom start out with the same difficulty in staying awake, the same vanilla questions they've been authorized to ask, the same confusion about why Miss America has come to talk to them and why they should care about what she has to say.

Eventually, the lead-up to these school visits becomes the most predictable thing of all. I might be in suburban Florida or rural Indiana or inner-city Des Moines, but the conversations are eerily similar. Almost always, I have a sit-down with the principal before the assembly. And very rarely—although it does happen, and I'm always grateful for it—does that principal say anything like "tell them what-ever you want. Our kids really need to hear about safer sex and AIDS."

Nope, most of the time it just doesn't work that way. It's me, my traveling companion du jour, and a (usually ner-vous) man in a suit and tie. Before he introduces me to his students, he's obligated to let me know that while they're thrilled to have me visit with their kids, HIV/AIDS is a topic that has raised some concerns in the past few days. "You see," this well-intentioned person will typically go on to say, "we really don't have a problem with that kind of thing here. Our kids are good, they graduate and go to college, they're involved in lots of extracurricular activities, and the best thing you can do is encourage them to study hard and chase their dreams like you did." Or something like that. Again and again.

And see, the first few times, it really scares the hell out of me. I mean, who do I think I am, introducing something like AIDS to a bunch of seventeen-year-olds, or fourteen-year-olds, or ten-year-olds? It's a wake-up call. I mean, you can read all the statistics you want about middle-schoolers hav-ing sex (which they do, in incredibly worrisome numbers), but when you actually stand up in front of a room full of them, it seems impossible to believe. Because they just look so small. It's shocking to think that they're already at risk for all kinds of things that threaten their lives. It's even more nerve-wracking to stand outside an auditorium, waiting to be introduced. Because they're inside hoping you brought your crown, and you're hoping you don't spend the next forty-five minutes killing a piece of their innocence. The butterflies always rampage through my stomach at such moments.

The principals don't just give gentle hints, either. They hand me lists. Lists of words I can't say, topics I shouldn't discuss, messages their kids don't need to hear. The most vivid example of this is the one I've spoken of most often: sit-

*ting on a plane from San Francisco to South Carolina, re-
viewing both the state and the district guidelines on what I
cannot say at the schools where I'll be speaking. Like everyone, of course, they're happy to have me. And they know I'm
traveling the country talking about AIDS. But in the course
of doing so on their turf, I am not allowed to say "condom."
I can't say "gay" or "straight" or "lesbian," not even to discuss the history of the epidemic. Can't get into the high rates
of transmission attributed to the dirty hypodermic needles
passed around by IV drug users. Can't talk about sex too
much, either, because all they teach is abstinence until marriage. Sidebar: If you're an educator or city council member
or parent and you're reading this, you should know that abstinence-only education is an enormous waste of taxpayer
money, with only minimal anecdotal evidence that it ever,
ever works. Comprehensive sex education that includes abstinence talk has consistently proven to be much more effective at reducing risk without increasing sexual activity
rates among teenagers. So . . . that.*

*In the beginning, I chicken out more often than not. I start
to think that maybe I'm the crazy one. That maybe the statistics are incorrect. Or that the numbers are skewed by inner-city kids going at it like rabbits, while the kids in small
Texas towns really do put it off until they get to the honeymoon suite. And then one day I'm on a rural road in mid-
dle-of-nowhere Illinois, sitting in the back of a car and waiting for the stoplight to change. As I'm thinking about all
this, I'm looking out the window at the red pickup that's just
screeched to a halt beside our stretch limo. The girl in the
driver's seat can't be older than seventeen. Bleached blonde
hair. Music blasting. A row of piercings up the ear that I can
see, and a couple of tattoos on the arm that's hanging out the
open window, so she can hold her cigarette.*

Huh.

*It may sound like a small thing, but it's about as pro-
nounced a eureka moment as I've had. And I start really*

paying attention to the kids, and figure out pretty quickly that they want *to ask about a lot more than whether I have a boyfriend or what kind of car I drive. The more I talk to them like equals—the more I think of myself as a peer educator instead of a pageant winner from on high—the more they come out of their shells and ask the tough questions.*

And again, it almost always happens the same way. It gets to the point where I literally agree to anything the principals ask in what I've come to think of as our sinister little meetings. Don't say condom? Sure. Don't talk about gay people? You got it. After a couple months, I probably would consent to avoid using the letter "w" as much as humanly possible. As long as I offhandedly slip in one polite question before I leave that room. See, I can happily agree to their terms, as long as they're cool with the fact that I need to have an open forum when we get to the question-and-answer portion. I'm perfectly fine with not mentioning any of their designated dirty words, but if the students ask about those things, I want the administration's blessing to answer honestly. Not one single decision maker ever turns down my request. Usually they laugh it off; they're so sure that their kids won't ask anything improper, that they aren't involved in any of that stuff, that they're going to be on their best behavior, that they've never even thought about sex.

Jackpot.

Once I figure this part out, school assemblies are a blast and a half. I give my speech, they ask questions. And as I get bolder, I start to drop hints into my speech to provoke their questions. I mean, if you use the word "protection" a few times, you haven't technically broken any of the agreed-upon rules, right? And when the kids later ask you what you mean by "protection," and you say "condoms," isn't that what the principal has agreed to regarding a no-holds-barred Q&A? Sure, I totally game the system. But what else am I supposed to do? Give a boring, condescending, up-on-a-pedestal speech that provides no information beyond "just say no" and "follow your dreams," when that type of evasion is exactly what's causing AIDS to spread faster and faster and faster? I mean, if you see a sixteen-year-old standing in the street, with his back to a Mack truck that's barreling toward him, do you really want to be the loser who doesn't yell, "Hey! Look out for that truck!"

I tell them that they can ask me absolutely anything. And boy, do they. Usually the questions start out pretty mildly: how I got into pageants, where I grew up. But I'm always waiting. Because I've now learned that in almost every group of kids, regardless of size, there's one hotshot—usually a boy—who wants to put you on the spot. Not so much to embarrass you (or so I like to think) as to impress his friends and make everybody laugh. I love That Kid. He works as the icebreaker to get into the real, important questions. I definitely have to earn my stripes each time, but once the kids figure out that I can hang, and that I'm not going to run out of the room or start crying (and especially when I'm a bit of a smart-ass right back), the floodgates open. Over the course of the year, That Kid asks about everything from oral sex to—true story—what he should do about a yellow-green rash on his scrotum (here's where I should mention the fact that That Kid is also The Kid Most Likely To Get Dragged Out Of An Assembly By The Vice-Principal).

That Kid asks a lot of questions about my own sex life, which is the hardest topic to navigate. I don't want to make headlines for my sexual proclivities; more important, I have a gut feeling that it's crucial not to alienate the kids who aren't making the same choices I do. In truth, at this point, I've never had sex. I've never even been close to sex. But the phantom headline "Virgin Miss America Gives AIDS Talk at Area School" haunts my nightmares. It's nobody's business, and more than that, it has the potential to backfire in about five different ways. So in the end, I steal a line from Leanza Cornett (1993) and say that I practice what I preach. Or that I've never had unsafe sex. There's no information

in that answer, of course, but they're almost always satis-
fied with it. All of this stuff acts as a springboard for discus-
sion—and, probably, as a cause of skyrocketing blood pres-
sure among the grown-ups standing around the room, whose
proud smiles fade once they hear some of the stuff coming
out of their little angels' mouths in front of Miss America.
They shouldn't have worried—I couldn't be happier. Good-
bye, stupid questions about swimsuits; hello, questions that
could save a teenager's life.

It's a high when I succeed at those assemblies. It's a high
afterward, too, because if they aren't forced to go back to
class right away, the kids hang around and talk to me. Some
of them want a photo (in hindsight, I'm so glad these are the
days before every cell phone has a camera). But some stay
to say the kinds of things you just can't say in front of your
whole school. Many times, they have a friend or family mem-
ber with HIV and don't know how to deal with it. One sweet,
pretty, Midwestern cheerleader-type tells me that her best
friend has just tested positive and is trying to figure out how
to tell her parents. Another confides that she's been thinking
about having sex with her boyfriend, but after hearing me
speak, she's decided to wait. This happens more than once,
and it always makes me really happy, because I'm not an ab-
stinence-pusher. Do I talk about it? Absolutely. But never,
I like to think, do I orient a speech from the perspective of
you-shouldn't-do-this-but-oh-well-if-you-have-to-I-guess-
there's-some-stuff-you-should-know. For me, it's always
about options, not caving to peer pressure, being okay with
going against the crowd, and protecting yourself every sin-
gle time you get into a situation that might put you at risk.

Because I do it this way, trying hard not to advocate or
judge, I learn something amazing and heartening: there is
absolutely every reason to believe that teenagers are capa-
ble of making smart, healthy choices if they're given accu-
rate and complete information. Sometimes I don't know how
to answer their questions, of course... but I believe that Miss

America, aside from being a public servant, also needs to be a traffic cop. It's fine to show up somewhere and stir everything up, but you'd better remember that you're leaving the next day. It would be wildly irresponsible for me not to educate myself in advance about the resources in the cities and towns I visit. I try to help them figure out where to go after I leave—plenty of times, I just recommend that they talk to their parents or the guidance counselor, but I also make the kids repeat the National HIV/AIDS Hotline number during the assembly. Ethically speaking, I know I can't just go in, talk to them, accept their school sweatshirt or the key to the city, and sail blithely back to the airport without helping them locate the network of resources available to them. It's now that I also become a big fan of peer educators: I have absolutely no problem with an entire school bypassing the drivel that's shoveled at them by teachers who are either naive or forbidden to talk turkey about sex and health. As long as the one kid in school who knows where to get condoms is properly trained and can dole out accurate information, that kid is an invaluable resource.

In my perfect world, comprehensive health education curriculum (including the truth about safer sex) would be legislatively mandated starting in middle school. And at the appropriate grade level, students would be able to go get condoms—and counseling—in the school nurse's office. But that seems about as likely as hell freezing over, so if the condoms are in somebody's locker, fine by me. As long as anyone who takes one knows to check its expiration date, stay away from oil-based lubricants that break down the latex, keep it out of their wallet so it doesn't deteriorate, avoid layering them (or, to use everyone's favorite slang, "double bagging"), and so on. Condoms are not, by nature, all that difficult to figure out—but they sure don't do much good if you use them incorrectly.

Those assemblies aren't the only high that comes from doing something that matters. I love when a really great op-ed piece or news story comes out. Don't get me wrong—there is a definite law of diminishing returns when it comes to having my picture in the paper. But every so often, a really kick-ass piece appears, focusing not on the crown or what I'm wearing, but on the fact that Miss America is transforming, and I'm helping her to do so. There's only one that I actually frame, from the Boston Globe, *both because the writing is so beautiful and because the author, James Carroll, homes in on exactly what I want so badly to achieve. I'm not a sappy girl, but I'll tell you what: this one still makes my eyes well up a little bit.*

Instead of serving as a consumer culture icon of loveliness, she has made her own the cause of the most despised among us. Instead of adopting the sex-symbol style of demure coyness, Shindle speaks frankly about the need for sex education in high schools, including condoms. Instead of denigrating women by enacting male fantasies of beauty, Shindle has been a defender of women who are being infected by the AIDS virus at rates never seen before. Instead of remaining aloof, unpolitical, and noncontroversial, she has decried the federal government's refusal to fund the very needle-exchange programs that federal research shows to be successful in stemming AIDS and even getting addicts into treatment.

It is stunning to attach such words to the pretty face of the girl I watched, as she listened to the teenage volunteers. Kate Shindle has the figure-perfect, wholesome "beauty" of a contest winner, but there is a depth in her dark eyes that suggests another kind of beauty. She is alive to the pain of America's young people—because she is one of them.

I saw Miss America use the peculiar power that came her way this year to soothe that pain in teenagers who, like her, have chosen for each other's sake to feel it. If Miss America has taken on such a cause; if young America can

*produce such a beauty whose best features are courage and
compassion, then hope is alive.*

It's amazing what happens when that momentum gets
rolling. The first story that really grabs me is Marc Pey-
ser's piece in Newsweek. He and I have spent World AIDS
Day together; it's intense. No matter how together you believe yourself to be (or how nice they are), being trailed by a
thinking, attentive journalist can be intimidating. We sit in
the connecting living room in my J. W. Marriott hotel suite
that evening so that I can answer his questions. But I'm also
trying to anticipate the land mines before they blow up in
plain sight of millions of readers. When Marc's piece comes
out, it's a big deal; although other journalists have given me
favorable coverage, this one has a lot of nuance and insight.
And of course, the Newsweek imprimatur is valuable. After
that, I'm more likely to have a quote from one of my speeches
hit the wire service, more likely to be the subject of interesting editorials, more likely to be given too much credit for
having some killer media strategy. In reality, I'm just going where I'm told and following my gut regarding what to
say when I get there. But the impression it's making on the
public consciousness begins to pile up in a really significant way.

The same is true of awards. I still laugh about the fact
that after I receive one from a major HIV/AIDS organization, they whisper in my ear that the other possible honor-
ees in contention had been Vice President and Mrs. Gore.
Heady stuff for someone who's barely old enough to order
her own beer at a restaurant. I get some beautiful things and
some very, very meaningful ones. But the real prize, as far
as I'm concerned, is always the ability to win respect for the
Miss America Organization. Generally, the audience at an
AIDS service organization's awards gala is already sym-
pathetic to the cause. But they're often very skeptical of the
pageant. I am keenly and constantly aware that the speeches

I give on these occasions (and at other similar high-profile events, like the World AIDS Conference and the National Press Club) are high risk, high reward. Sometimes I get a last-minute burst of inspiration from what's already been said that night and scribble a supplemental paragraph on my napkin, or rewrite the whole speech at the bottom of the menu or on a torn-out page from the evening's program. Every time I stand behind a podium to be recognized, I grab for the brass ring that I believe will help lead Miss America back to cultural relevance. Who really cares about me? In a matter of months, they will crown a new winner and put me out to pasture. But in the meantime, I'm absolutely determined to elevate Miss America. At the time, it's not only an organization doing something nobody else is doing—giving a college student a prominent national platform for social activism—but all the old jokes and condescending one-liners that have hounded Miss America for decades just seem totally played out.

For a while, it works. Boy, does it work. I'm getting to do the most stimulating and challenging work I've ever done, at the very highest levels that exist. Because I'm dedicated, because I take advantage of every opportunity that seems even peripherally substantive, I find myself on the inside track of something I care deeply about. When President Clinton makes the disappointing decision to oppose federal funding for lifesaving needle exchange programs, I get a heads-up call from Secretary Donna Shalala's Health and Human Services office just before the news goes public. I remember being in yet another indistinguishable hotel room, my hair wet, trying to iron my clothes for that day's appearances, and HHS is suddenly on the line for me. Somehow I find myself "in the loop," as they say.

All this is not to say that there aren't bumps in the road. Of course there are. I have to fight (and then write a proposal, and then fight some more) to be able to do a little volunteer work on the side. I do get tired of standing behind a podium all the time, when my background has been so varied. More than that, though, I believe that it's good for the pageant if the public sees Miss America getting her hands dirty, instead of just making speeches and shaking hands with people in suits. The Miss America staff doesn't see it that way. They're worried that the sponsors bringing me to town will be angry if my stop at a soup kitchen poaches media attention from the bigger events I'm there to promote. I keep the debate alive, and eventually, I win. I work in a couple of food pantries. I chop broccoli at a soup kitchen. To my knowledge, no one ever complains—mostly because I'm careful to direct attention back to the main event that's brought me to town in the first place.

Things are going well for me, but they're also going well for those who have been fighting HIV/AIDS for a long time. Throughout the year, there is tremendous optimism about the future of the epidemic. The new protease inhibitor "cocktail"—so named because it involves a combination of different drugs attacking the virus from different angles—seems to be extending both the length and the quality of life for people with AIDS. AZT, which has had mixed results for many years (and is still the only affordable treatment for most of the developing world) has been mostly phased out in America. The cocktail isn't a miracle, but it's far better than the death sentence AIDS has been for years. And the HIV/AIDS movement (initially launched as a desperate plea for the world to notice that otherwise healthy people had started dropping dead) is by this point a model of health-related activism. Sure, we might eventually look back at it as the initiative that launched a thousand colored lapel ribbons. But it has also launched a thousand nonviolent protests that make use of shocking imagery, the way ACT UP did when they lay in the street covered in fake blood. Or put a giant condom over Jesse Helms's house. Or—well—did anything Larry Kramer participated in.

But, of course, the year isn't all sunshine and unicorns.

I certainly have access and make inroads because of the crown in my suitcase. There are some things, though, that are insurmountable for me. No matter what I'm able to achieve, there are plenty of times when I learn that I simply can't help. As excited as everyone is about the protease inhibitors, for example, they definitely have their flaws. I meet people who tell me about the difficulties of getting—and staying on—these drugs. Those living with HIV/AIDS are taking up to sixty pills every single day, with significant restrictions regarding their use. Some need to be taken on an empty stomach. Some require fatty foods. Many have to be refrigerated, making it more and more difficult to treat the communities seeing massive increases in infection rates: the poor, the homeless, the indigent. HIV isn't a thinking virus, of course, but it's about as close to "smart" as a disease gets; it mutates so quickly that missing a few doses, or taking a drug holiday, can allow the disease to quickly become resistant to medications that were previously effective.

Even under the best of circumstances, assuming 100 percent compliance with a drug regimen, living with HIV/AIDS long term has never been easy. Some of the drugs are so toxic that they're far from a panacea. Ultimately, they end up simply being a moderate extension of life for many people. Uncle Bob is a perfect example: after several years of treatment, his kidneys just can't take it anymore. The same medications that promise to save him eventually kill him. In 1999, when I see him alive for the last time, the whites of his eyes are so yellow that they look like they've been colored in with a crayon.

And as awkward a comparison as it may be, the Miss America Organization is still facing significant limitations of its own. Yes, several Miss Americas have been able to achieve major advancements in terms of respect and relevance. But while we can treat the symptoms of what ails the pageant, we can't cure it, any more than the best doctors in the world can cure the HIV/AIDS epidemic. For a long time,

I believe we can—if only I work hard enough. I want the country to see the institution the way I see it—full of opportunity, full of influence, limitless in its potential.

It's such a dangerous thing to fall in love with potential. Doing so—whether it's a person or an entity—is basically a fast track to getting your heart broken. Until 1995, for example, Chevrolet is a major sponsor of Miss America. And in many frustrating ways, trying to save Miss America proves to be a lot like restoring a '57 Chevy. You can give it a new paint job, rebuild the engine, replace the cloth top, and on and on and on. But there are so many moving parts to keep track of, and if one isn't working perfectly, it can drag down the whole enterprise. I will learn this, painfully and repeatedly, later. And then again. And again. Until I finally realize that if Miss America herself is one of the very few pushing the Chevy uphill, she'd better eventually figure out when to get out of the way, before it rolls backwards and crushes her under its wheels.

With or without the silver bullet of a platform issue, it was crazy to think that I could save Miss America. But, oh, how I tried.

TEN

During the last decade of the twentieth century, the Miss America Organization (as it had officially been rechristened) made major changes. Some were smart, some were shortsighted, and some were just downright desperate. But with each passing year (and as ratings for the annual telecast consistently fell), the pageant was at least making efforts to rebrand itself.

With the new-car smell barely wearing off of his term as CEO, Leonard Horn decided to bring in a new executive producer for the pageant. Starting in 1993, the pageant gradually relegated longtime producer Bill Caligari to preliminary-night duties, while Emmy winner Jeff Margolis took over as both producer and director.

Clearly, one of the goals of Margolis and his team was to shake up the format of the show. For years, if not decades, the pageant had followed essentially the same pattern: introduce the contestants, introduce the host(s), narrow the field to a top ten to compete in swimsuit, talent, and evening gown, and announce the runners-up and the winner. Sure, there were small alterations here and there. Sometimes the winner was called from a field of six (the four runners-up having already been announced and the rest of the top ten waiting with bated breath); in other years, the ten were first narrowed to a top five. For a few years, the top *two* were plucked out of the final seven (after the weeding-out of the fourth, third, and second runners-up), keeping the field as large as possible for as long as possible before surrendering to the higher-drama visual of the Last Two Standing. But in general, the show had largely remained unchanged for much of its lifetime on television.

Margolis was proactive. During his seven-year stint, he and pageant officials tinkered with numerous elements of the format. Almost immediately, the production numbers became more current. The music that accompanied them was more contemporary, but not awkwardly so, and every-one spent less time lip-syncing along with prerecorded tracks. The contestants themselves—for better or, some-times, worse—were involved as singers and dancers, some-times in elaborate outfits (in one number, they wore cos-tumes made largely of inflated balloons).

The early nineties also saw the introduction of new em-cees for the show. After surviving an agonizing eleven-minute delay just before the crowning of Miss America 1989—and here, one must really refer to William Goldman's *Hype and Glory* for the most painfully detailed account of that night's events—Gary Collins was replaced by popular morning show hosts Regis Philbin and Kathie Lee Gifford.

The biggest evolution during the 1990s, at least in terms of scoring, was the gradual shortening of the talent com-petition. A word about talent: although it has almost al-ways been the highest-value competition, the judges are of-ten reminded that the contestants are not expected to be professional-level entertainers. Still, no thinking person should argue that the overall quality of talent hasn't been spotty in the past two decades. Part of that was due to the simple fact that more women were choosing to go to college to pursue non-artistic careers, and just had fewer hours to practice the piano. But also, the contestant's charisma and spokesperson skills (as demonstrated in the private interview) became more and more important in an era when Miss America was chasing both institutional and platform-related credibility. Talent may have been responsible for more *actual* points, but a good interview could scatter de facto points across all of the competitions.

Also, while the platform issue took center stage—requiring a significant time commitment to community service and activism—the opportunities for talented young women to use Miss America as a launching pad for entertainment careers were waning. Miss America herself now spent more time on Capitol Hill than at Carnegie Hall; her prize package included scholarships instead of screen tests. Young women who were seeking to perform at the highest artistic levels undoubtedly began to wonder whether the pageant was a legitimate outlet for introducing themselves to the entertainment industry—or if it was just a lot of trouble for a diminishing amount of screen time and artistic cred. In the 1978 finals, for example, talent was worth one-third of the contestant's score—the same value as swimsuit and evening gown—and she demonstrated her skills, such as they were, for two minutes and fifty seconds; that year's Miss Washington went almost a full three minutes. In 1993, the performances were shortened to two minutes, thirty seconds; in 1996, they went to a flat two minutes. The year 1999 was the first in which only the top five contestants performed talent. And by the time Miss America was dropped from network television after the 2004 pageant, the talent competition had been reduced to a "showdown" between the top two; although both women were well-rounded and consistent across the categories, neither gave a particularly stellar performance. Although he had left his CEO duties in 1998, the always-outspoken Horn offered some typically pointed words regarding this turn of events. He essentially blamed the cheese factor on local and state volunteers who had just been around too

long, flatly stating that "the talent got homogenous and boring" and that "by the time (the contestants) reach the national level they no longer look like fresh girls or 21-year-
olds. They look like 40-year-old Stepford Wives. If they are
going to relate to the women in audience, they have to look
and act like their peers."

The leadership's basic reasoning behind the Incredi-
ble Shrinking Talent Competition was that most of the talents weren't strong enough to be showcased in an era when
attention spans were getting shorter and television re-
motes would be used liberally across America as soon as
a singer hit a bad note. The enormous and sustained success of *American Idol* just a couple of years later seems to
disprove this hypothesis; clearly, America was just fine
with tuning in to watch terrible singers sing terribly. Perhaps the disparity in ratings can be attributed to the fact
that *Idol* clearly delineated between good and bad, or that
Idol judges weren't compelled to heap flattery on anyone—
even their best singers—after a poor showing. But because
Miss America contestants were consistently treated with
reverence regardless of their performance quality (and
one could argue that their achievements, if not their entertainment abilities, warranted such treatment), the pageant
didn't offer the kind of gleeful schadenfreude that televised
talent shows had, did, and would. In other words, no matter what happened with Miss Alaska's baton twirling, no
one was going to sound the gong. And no one was going to
tell her afterward that she had been terrible—at least, not
to her face. As the years went on, the swimsuits and gowns
continued to hold appeal, but viewers were more likely to
switch off the talent competition and return only for the
crowning moment at the end of the show.

All that aside, there were indeed substantive and positive changes in the show during the 1990s. The reintroduc-
tion of the top-five segment gradually brought the platform
issue into much sharper focus. Over the course of the de-

cade, the awkward memorized personal statements (usually delivered at a microphone during the evening gown
competition) disappeared entirely. Instead, the five finalists were asked to sit down with a host—Philbin, Nancy
Glass, *The View*'s Meredith Vieira—and answer questions
in a roundtable format. This moment, along with home videos and "up close and personal" features on each hopeful,
allowed the viewing audience to connect with more real,
relatable Miss America contestants. The glimpse of conversation also provided insight into each contestant's individual judges' interview. As the first of all the competitions, the private interview has a significant impact on the
outcome. But because it is only seen by the judging panel,
it can make for a head-scratching moment at the end of the
evening . . . especially if one or two of the women seem to
be miles ahead in the onstage competition, yet don't end up
with the crown. The refrain that "it must have been her interview" has been both grumbled and shouted joyfully all
over pageant venues for years following the announcement of the new Miss Whatever. Finally, the new Woman
of Achievement Award, given by Miss America to a distin-
guished female, was noted during the telecast. Usually, it
was a pre-taped segment with the recipient. First Ladies
Hillary Clinton (1995) and Barbara Bush (1997) and movie
star Sharon Stone (1998) were among the recipients, chosen on the basis of their humanitarian efforts—sometimes
in the field of Miss America's platform, sometimes for their
broader philanthropic work.

Developments like these certainly highlighted the evolution of the pageant. But the largest challenge—and one
that has never quite been met—was synchronizing the
telecast with the day-to-day duties of the winner herself. Miss America's "year of service" (a phrase that uni-
laterally replaced the outdated "reign") changed significantly in the 1990s. While the organization continued to
use the same statistic (actually calculated by Miss Amer-

ica 1990, Debbye Turner, during some downtime with her traveling companion): at least 20,000 miles a month in domestic and (occasionally) international travel, the focus of those trips shifted. The new Miss America was quickly and strategically aligned with nonprofit and corporate entities that shared her stated mission. Often, these groups would seek her out, recruiting her to travel to their fundraisers, lobbying efforts, and educational initiatives. As a result, about 80 to 90 percent of her year was spent doing real boots-on-the-ground advocacy and education, with the remaining time dedicated to sponsor appearances, autograph sessions, and selected performances. In the 1990s, Miss America evolved from a figurehead to an activist, turning the spotlight away from herself and onto an issue she felt was critical. In terms of mainstream legitimacy, it was arguably the pageant's most important initiative since the introduction of scholarships. The platform issue was strongly emphasized in Miss America's marketing materials. In the national program book, for example, it slid neatly into the spot where the contestants' eye color and measurements had once been printed.

But was it sexy television? For a while, it was different enough to take center stage. The top five competition focused almost exclusively on platform. Although it was initially met with skepticism or derision—critics snarked about hearing "beauty queens" play concertos and wax poetic about literacy—there was, as the decade progressed, evidence that Miss America's efforts were indeed penetrating the public consciousness. Even author Sarah Banet-Weiser recognized the shifting identity that Miss America was trying to carve out for herself. Though she remained skeptical of the throwback "nurturing" element of many of the platform issues, she asserted that "the politics of the Miss America pageant dovetail with early, first-wave liberal feminism in the United States. [Miss America] consistently and forcefully establishes herself as an icon of respectability, someone much more than a mere beauty queen."

There were certainly obstacles on the way to this new identity. Carolyn Sapp (1992) competed with a platform of education, but quickly found her year sidetracked when her past came back to haunt her. Shortly after her crowning, the media uncovered that she had been involved in a physically abusive relationship with an NFL player; Sapp soon became a de facto spokesperson for domestic violence organizations. Leanza Cornett (1993) was widely praised for her HIV/AIDS platform, especially since the disease directly affected such a large segment of the pageant's volunteer network. However, her devotion to her advocacy led her to violate one of the most sacrosanct traditions among Miss America's most faithful fans: she decided that she would not wear the crown when making appearances, claiming that it undercut her credibility as an activist. Her actions would eventually point up a major philosophical split between old- and new-school pageant fans. The former group openly threatened to boo her on the Convention Hall stage the year she crowned her successor, and opined that her first runner-up would probably be more than happy to show up in Atlantic City for those few final days and wear whatever headpiece she was asked to. The latter group recognized the cognitive dissonance that Cornett was pointing out ("How do you talk about practicing safe sex when you've got this thing on top of your head?" she asks), but were still far outnumbered by the traditionalists.

As the platform issue became more dominant, some of the pageant faithful began to express displeasure with what they saw as a new breed of winner: savvy and well-spoken above all, worldly, and less calculatedly glamorous than she had been in the past. Miss America was being redefined; she may have still been "the girl next door," but she was leaning away from head-cheerleader status and more toward that of a thoughtful valedictorian. Of course, sell-

ing this evolving image to the public required a complicated equation. Plenty of the pageant's previously tolerable
quirks suddenly appeared to be completely anachronistic—
not the least of which was the continuation of the much-
maligned swimsuit competition. For better or for worse,
whether explained in terms of tradition, health and well-
being, or fitness, the concept of young women parading in
swimsuits in order to win college scholarships remained a
thorn in the pageant's side. Numerous Miss Americas expressed discomfort with that part of the competition; Cornett, Heather Whitestone (1995), and Heather French
(2000) have strongly implied that it should be eliminated
from the judging criteria. Even CEO Leonard Horn consistently regarded it with trepidation . . . although he liked to
ride the fence when it came to actual action: "I would eliminate it tomorrow if it wouldn't jeopardize the television
audience," Horn is reported to have said. "But I've been
warned not to get rid of it by the so-called experts."

Indeed, the most relentlessly pursued target during the
Horn/Margolis years was the swimsuit competition. Seeking once and for all to bang the cultural gavel on the issue,
the 1995 pageant incorporated a viewer call-in vote to decide whether this portion of the show would even happen.
The well-spun effort—in which the powers that be claimed
to be interested in letting the public make the determina
tion about swimsuits—was actually a ringer; the cost of
each phone vote virtually guaranteed that the pageant's
fans would dial in greater numbers than its detractors. And
they did. About a million viewers spent fifty cents for each
vote. Seventy-nine percent of them gave the thumbs-up to
the swimsuit competition; since that decisive moment, it
has continued without many mea culpas.

For three years, citing the more "natural" look that Miss
America was striving for, pageant officials banned high
heels with the swimsuits, creating an even stranger pro-
cession of women who gently tiptoed in an arched-foot

Barbie-esque manner, lest flatly clomping around cause any unsightly jiggling. In 1997, contestants were instructed to buy swimsuits off the rack, allegedly to encourage individuality and phase out the era of the heavy-duty, one-piece, girdle-esque "supersuit." That same year, for the first time in five decades, the two-piece swimsuit was permitted back on the Miss America stage . . . a mere thirty-seven years after a memorably itsy-bitsy yellow version made its way into mainstream consciousness courtesy of Brian Hyland. And in a moment that must have broken records for cultural tone deafness, the 1998 contestants paraded up a short flight of stairs and stood on a platform that slowly spun them around to be viewed from all angles. Presumably, the intent was not to portray them like the desserts one sees in those rotating glass cases in diners across America. Nevertheless, the similarity was certainly observed and dissected in many quarters.

Swimsuits notwithstanding, the pageant seemed to be gaining a new foothold by the end of the decade, occupying sturdier ground than it had in many years. Miss America was routinely recognized for her work with her platform issue; to a great extent, her focus as an activist permitted each winner to be more clearly and specifically defined than she would have been in earlier years. The inclusion of the platform issue meant that the pageant could become less dependent on the personality traits and individual charisma of the annual winner. From day one, there was automatically a press hook (and usually an accompanying personal story) for each new Miss America, and it went far beyond whether she'd brought her pet crab to the press conference.

Over time, the trickle-down effect catalyzed noticeable change in the type of young woman who decided to compete for titles at every level. Horn seemed to understand that a community service initiative wouldn't change the image of Miss America all by itself; it had to be accompa-

nied by the evolution of policy, visual imagery, and vocabu-
lary. So he made across-the-board tweaks to long-standing
practices, as is apparent in one volunteer's 1998 summary
of the period: "Today's contestants are more mature, goal-
oriented, independent young women than those I worked
with in the '70s. Banners and rosettes were discontinued,
the image of the crown was played down, and words such
as 'crowning,' 'reign' and 'girls' were no longer used in pub-
lications. The contestants now arrive in Atlantic City
wearing business attire instead of cocktail attire, the cover
photo of the Pageant program book features Miss America in business or casual attire and since 1997, contestants
over 21 are even permitted to visit casinos."

Additionally, the majority of Miss Americas—who, after all, were constantly on the road, absorbing both praise
and criticism that was often beyond their control—seemed
to welcome this emphasis on brains over physical beauty.
Many, if not most, outgoing winners wore their activism as
a more significant badge of honor than their actual pageant
victory, and almost all remained substantially involved
with their chosen causes well past the end of their terms.
The cumulative effect of the platform era has been repeatedly cited by contestants at all levels as an enabler of access and respectability that had eluded their predecessors,
as Tara Dawn Holland (1997) articulated after passing on
her crown. "It changed literally every aspect of my life,"
she recalled a few years later. "Before I was Miss America I
wrote to officials about literacy, but never got any interest.
But when I won, everyone wanted to talk to me. They listened because of that fake crown."

In addition to the value the platform issue added for the
individual Miss Americas, the pageant as a whole could begin to dig itself out from decades of skepticism. Miss America was no longer celebrated merely for winning a contest.
She had a body of work that could be marketed, and it went
far further than a stereotypical call for world peace. Al-

though sponsors still came and went, the Miss America Organization began to build a new brand. As Horn put it, the very essence of the program had undergone a critical shift. At the end of his CEO term, he contended that the pageant was "no longer about a silly beauty contest. Now, she's a relevant, socially responsible activist. . . . When I took over, the pageant was practically broke, irrelevant and unimportant, and Miss America was dismissed as no more than just another wholesome American woman from Podunk, who would open for politicians, sell sponsors' products or cut the ribbons at shopping malls. That we've survived the most difficult years in the pageant's history is no accident. So don't talk to me about two-piece swimsuits."

Finally, and critically, when Horn retired in 1998, he left the Miss America Organization in fairly sound financial shape. Having built up a rainy-day fund of nearly $10 million (from basically no cash reserve at the beginning of his term) and what seemed like a promising relationship with ABC (after longtime network NBC dropped the telecast in 1997), it seemed that for the first time in a long time, Miss America was on the precipice of calling her own shots.

But that's the thing about the precipice: it's tough to tell, before you take that next step, whether you're going to soar or come crashing back down to earth.

A magical evening on the beach with Nancy Chapman, Miss Oklahoma 1982. If Miss America ambition is contagious, this was definitely the moment I caught it. Author's collection.

I dare you to spot the future Miss America in this eighth-grade class picture. Author's collection.

*After winning a small local pageant to
become Miss Lake-Cook 1997, I had my state
headshot done at the Glamour Shots in a
nearby suburban mall. Author's collection.*

*Rehearsing (with dreamy Miss America dancer Bob Gaynor)
for the evening gown competition. Author's collection.*

... a few hours later, it was time for the real thing. Author's collection.

I will never understand why "pageant people" hated this swimsuit.
I just thought it was cool. Donald B. Kravitz/DBK Photo.

And then . . . Donald B. Kravitz/DBK Photo.

As Miss America 1998, I gave speeches. And speeches,
and speeches, and speeches. Here I am with Denver
mayor Wellington Webb. Author's collection.

Kids loved the crown. I was pretty sure they liked me too, but let's be honest: the girl in the white shirt isn't that excited about getting to meet me. *Spieth Photography.*

*Sans crown, I chatted with then-Senator
John Kerry... Author's collection.*

*... and somehow kept on smiling when Senator Strom
Thurmond got a little handsy. Author's collection.*

*By day, riding down Chicago's Michigan Avenue in a horse-drawn
carriage in the Brach's Holiday Parade. Author's collection.*

*That night, I caught up on sleep on the floor of O'Hare
International Airport. Author's collection.*

Is there life after Miss America? September in Atlantic City, for a former Miss America, is basically the equivalent of Cheers: everybody knows your name. In 2002, future Harvard Law student Erika Harold took the crown and posed with fifteen previous Miss Americas (I'm in the back row, far right.) Author's collection.

Part Three

THE UGLY PAGEANT

ELEVEN

Most of my year has passed before I get the unpleasant surprise of finding out what seemingly everybody thinks of me.

The late 1990s have been, to say the least, an explosive time for the Internet. My first exposure to it happens in my sophomore year in high school, when I look carefully at a syllabus in British lit class. The teacher, Ms. Cecil, lists an e-mail address as one of the ways to contact her, while cautioning that she only checks it "sporadically." E-mail, I remember thinking. What, exactly, is e-mail?

Not that I'm unfamiliar with computers. The trusty Apple IIc at home has brought many documents to life underneath my fingers. I've saved them to big floppy disks, secreting away the ones that contain my angst-y preteen poetry and—notably and somewhat embarrassingly—what would now be called "fan fiction" (which I then called "stories") about the New Kids on the Block. There is absolutely nothing racy about the stuff, but I am nonetheless terrified that someone in my family might discover my most precious, private flights of imagination. As far as documenting one's life, I'm part of the first generation who find typing to be a faster and clearer way of expressing myself than writing in long-

hand. All these years later, despite a more-than-adequate collection of typing skills classes, I still call myself the fastest two-finger typist I know. Which should probably be mortifying, but, hey, it works.

By the time I get to college, the Internet has been growing at a steady pace. There aren't websites, exactly, but there's something called a listserv where people gather virtually to trade information. The 1995 Sandra Bullock movie The Net, *in which computer pros execute tasks that can now probably be done by most twelve-year-olds on a smartphone, blows my mind with the scale and scope of its technology. I'm a sophomore in college when it's released.*

So it really doesn't occur to me to check the Internet when I start to have success in pageants as a college junior.

After I actually become Miss America, I live most of the year in blissful ignorance. Sure, I occasionally check the daily paper in whatever town I might be visiting, to see what the media's absorbed from my activities. Usually, the most appalling thing is how the reporter in question has misquoted me; I take great care with grammar, etc., lest the media have an opportunity to brand me with the same bimbo-airhead stereotype that has plagued every Miss America since before I was born. Our daily and monthly schedules arrive by fax, or as hard copies overnighted to the hotel. Aside from checking my personal AOL account and writing speeches, the only time I regularly spend on my laptop is when I bust out my tissue-box-sized printer to create thank-you notes on personalized stationery.

Then I find the chat rooms.

I'm not sure why I go looking in the first place. I may have typed my name into a search engine out of curiosity; after all, there are enough websites by this time that report the news. Plugging my name into one of them is probably a smart idea. I'm keenly aware that there's a fine line between effectiveness and irrelevance, between success and skep-

ticism. It makes sense to keep tabs on as much chatter as possible.

But what I find completely deflates my twenty-one-year-old cache of optimism and satisfaction. They—and I'm not sure who "they" are, only that they have a long history with pageants and, presumably, access to an ethernet port—find me lacking.

It's humiliating. The people who feel like I shouldn't have won . . . in fact, some of them think that because of my family's background as Miss America volunteers, I cheated to win. The people who think I'm a terrible singer, that I looked "like a man in drag" on the biggest night of my life (when actually I looked in the mirror and, for once, liked what I saw). That the first runner-up should have beaten me without breaking a sweat. That I'm the beginning of the end of the pageant, regardless of the thousands of hours I've spent trying to do good things that continue to build Miss America's legacy. It's like a fever dream come to life. In black and white, for the world to see, stated with purpose and certainty by the anonymous masses.

I spend a few days trying to defuse it. But the reality— and truly, a word to the wise here—is that there are few things more transparent than attempting to defend yourself, or your friend, or your kid, in a chat room or on a message board. If I spent some time, I could probably come up with a better explanation than Spidey Sense . . . but really, that's what it amounts to. The other, less genteel explanation is that it's like porn: you know it when you see it. The reasoning is too personal, the examples are too specific. It's actually painful to read the defenses of those who are just trying their best to convince someone (the greater pageant community? their state volunteers and boards of directors? themselves?) that they have worked hard and deserve . . . what? A crown? Credit for what they've accomplished? Acceptance? In every way that matters, it's a no-win situation, because the more you explain, the more they attack. Not all of them, of course; there are some nice people who post on these forums. There are some reasonable ones. There are some smart ones, with a talent for putting it all into perspective. Not that many, though. Given this knowledge, I cannot imagine what it's like to be famous—really famous, not Miss America famous— and have the circle of critics expand exponentially.

When I first learn that this community exists, I am properly horrified. Up to this point, I kind of think I've been totally killing it as Miss America, and expect that conventional wisdom agrees with me. As it turns out, not so much.

But thank God—and I really do thank God for this, because the alternative is almost too much to bear—I happen to be Miss America at the dawn of all this stuff. Because now, as opposed to then, the contestants who seek the biggest, sparkliest crown of all can log on at any time of the day or night. If they're so inclined, they can read what any random stranger thinks about their evening gown, the song they choose for talent, their lipstick or their hair color. Or whether they've let their roots grow in, or whether they've gained five pounds after the pageant. Or whether their face is symmetrical. Or their eye shadow is flattering. Or their dress for a particular event is tacky. Or that they "need" a nose job, have a weak chin, are too outspoken or too vanilla, should wear Spanx, should be ashamed to have to wear Spanx, need their eyebrows reshaped, have implants that are too obvious or cleavage that needs better support. It is the antithesis of what I hope Miss America will be. It is utterly useless and empowers no one.

These days, the young women who strive toward this goal don't just throw their respective hats into the ring and do their best. If they so choose—and no matter what anyone tells you, it's difficult to block it out—they can keep tabs on what everyone thinks about the choices they make. They never know who's behind a particular handle, or an anonymous post. It could be their runner-up from two years ago, or the runner-up's mom. It could be a board member who's cheering for someone else to win. Or a well-intentioned volunteer who wants a contestant to get herself together because she'd really be a great Miss State, if only she'd change her talent and her wardrobe and maybe get some lipo or Invisalign.

It disgusts me. But because it infuriates me, because it's a perversion of what Miss America should be and is inflicted upon young women who have stars in their eyes and no idea that they're actually signing up for this, it's hard to look away.

And so, since I have such trouble distancing myself from this type of preposterous yet mesmerizing criticism; because, despite my best efforts to compartmentalize and put things in perspective; despite the reassurance of friends and family that It Doesn't Matter and You're Doing Great and It Gets Better, I will tell you what it does to me.

First, a disclaimer: online message boards are not to blame for the choices I make. If I am to stretch, I might place accountability squarely on the identity crisis that pulls me, an average college student, in the opposite direction from me, the current Miss America. I might blame my control-freak control issues, in the context of a year when my life is not my own. I might point to the implied obligation to uphold an image that I never expected . . . although of course, with the benefit of age and hindsight, I know that I should have expected it.

In short, I get sick.

My issues with food and body image creep up on me. I truly haven't starved myself to be in swimsuit shape; I've worked my ass off to be fit and healthy. I've done push-up pyramids that turn my arms to Jell-O. I've eaten six times a day. Boring stuff, to be sure: grilled chicken, baked potatoes, salads, egg-white omelets, the slow, dull kind of oatmeal. I've learned that two-a-day workouts are my friend and junk food is my enemy. I know that there's a battalion of healthy choices when it comes to interesting foods, especially in the spice category. I've used enough liquid smoke and hot sauce to drown a New York subway rat.

This continues while I'm competing in Atlantic City. As a local, I have luxuries that other contestants do not. Although I'm not permitted to see him (lest some intrepid sleuth with press credentials leap to a scandalous conclusion), my dad drops off the primitive family exercise bike and a small microwave in my hotel room at the Claridge. Combined with my Abs of Steel video—and when I meet Abs of Steel guru Tamilee Webb a few years later at a San Diego fitness conference, I joyously announce that I never would have won Miss America without her—these tools keep me happy and healthy and fit. I pack a lunch each day: a can of low-sodium tuna, a baked potato, and one of the "good" fruits, like grapefruit ("bad" fruits, like bananas and grapes, are expected to sit in the corner and look ashamed of themselves). I ride that exercise bike at the end of the day. I do the abs video when I'm ready to fall asleep on the hotel floor, and elsewhere. If you have eagle eyes, you can watch my post-crowning victory walk and see the long bruise up my spine from doing crunches on the stage anytime there's five minutes between the end of lunch hour and the beginning of afternoon rehearsal.

And yet... and yet, when I become Miss America, it's suddenly not enough. With every chicken dinner, I feel like my sponsor-provided clothes get tighter. Despite the good work I know I'm doing, I worry that I'm letting people down. I take preemptive steps; when nonprofits call on me to cut the ribbons for their fund-raising AIDS Rides, I ask to participate. I spend my limited downtime in hotel gyms, following their trainer's helpful advice and riding the stationary bike for up to four hours at a time. I jump on a borrowed bike to do 100 miles from Chelsea Piers to Southampton. And then again, on the big island in Hawaii, 75 miles and a 4,000-foot climb up a volcano. I'm the first to finish in the female divi-

sion, mostly because I have to immediately fly back to Hono-lulu for a speech.

Quite simply, it is not enough.

I start to have problems with food. Without getting into the details, I'm overeating and then depriving myself. It's dangerous and stupid and utterly not who I am—but really, the fact that I do it basically does make it who I am. It's not unusual for me to burst into tears—big, hysterical tears, no less—if my plan to exercise gets thwarted by some event that runs long. Or if my ever-changing schedule means that I don't get back to the hotel until after the gym is closed. It's massively unhealthy, and it doesn't stop when I give up the crown.

My senior year is absolutely insane. I have one foot in fin-ishing my degree (and maintaining some kind of relation-ship with normalcy, like going to football games and do-ing college theater) and one foot in continuing the work I did as Miss America. It's not unheard of for me to miss classes on, say, a Tuesday, fly from O'Hare to DC, spend four or five hours meeting with legislators about HIV/AIDS issues, race to the airport to catch a three o'clock flight, and get back to campus just in time to make the evening rehearsal for a show I'm performing in. My professors are beyond understand-ing, particularly my acting teachers, who have been nothing but supportive of my platform work. But I'm stretched way too thin; something's gotta give. And so, even though I "have my life back" and can set my own schedule, my problems with food remain. In fact, they even intensify. The flip side of not having someone to do all my scheduling for me is that I have to learn to say no. It's so much easier to turn myself in-side out trying to make everyone happy—which, of course, is a fool's errand on its own.

All of this continues when I get to New York after grad-uation. I always hear that eating disorders are about con-trol, not food, and in my case, that's absolutely true. My guilt about not being able to please everyone combines with my trouble keeping my physical appearance at the highest possible level. I worry that no matter what I accomplish, those anonymous online phantoms still don't think I deserved to be Miss America, and I am determined to prove them wrong. On top of everything, I now live in a city where it seems like everyone is a size two (a physical impossibility for me because of my bone structure), and I'm trying to get off the ground in a business where one's appearance is literally part of the job description.

I run a marathon. I still don't like what I see in the mirror. I walk into a New York Sports Club and ask for the toughest trainer they have; they send me straight to Eytan. He makes me run sprints up the hill to Zabar's, and is kind of stoked on the day I almost throw up on the gym floor (let the record show that Eytan is awesome). I get a job in Jekyll and Hyde *on Broadway, and then I'm hired to star in the national tour of* Cabaret. *Back on the road. Again.*

I tell both actors and Miss Americas who are just starting out that if you have any demons, you can expect them to multiply like wet gremlins while you're touring. Mine certainly do. I absolutely love playing Sally Bowles, but dancing around in various types of lingerie—corsets and slips and stuff—for two hours a night kind of complicates things. My corset is custom-made for me; it fits like a glove and is incredibly flattering. As the months pass, I'm working out during the day, doing eight shows a week, and not eating all that much. For a while, I take metabolism-boosting energy supplements and drink a lot of coffee. Eventually, I'm not all that surprised when ephedrine gets pulled off the market; I figure there's something wrong the day I'm walking to the YMCA in Milwaukee and my heart starts fluttering in my chest. This freaks me out enough to ditch my bottle of Xenadrine, and then I gradually just kind of stop eating very much. It makes me feel great when my corset actually needs to be taken in. After about six months, I stop backstage at the still-running

Jekyll & Hyde *during a week off; I'm pumped to be asked how much weight I've lost and how I did it.*

A year later, I spend a few months in L.A. for pilot season, depressed for several reasons. First of all, I think Los Angeles is just fundamentally kind of a depressing place. Second, a particularly miserable breakup has rocked my self-esteem. And third, it's shortly after the September 11 attacks, which have knocked every New Yorker for a loop. I don't know many people there, so I have plenty of time to work out like a freak and skip meals left and right. Even with the muscle mass I accumulate, my weight keeps dropping until I'm about fifteen pounds thinner than I was during my televised swimsuit competition. I think I finally look great. But to this day, I still remember the look on my best friend's face when I take a weekend trip back to New York to see a show. He's not a fan of my new look.

Today, when I see pictures of myself from back then, it's hard to believe I could possibly have thought I was fat. My arms—never the easiest part of my body to keep in shape— are scary skinny. My jawline is sharp, the skin pulled tight. I don't look pretty by a long shot, but I remember feeling happy. Once I've learned that it makes me feel powerful to spend the day hungry (which is embarrassing even to admit to myself), I feel full in a different way. Feeling in control of my life or, at least, my appearance—is like a drug.

I never get to rock bottom in the same way that lots of people do. I never end up in the hospital, my hair doesn't fall out, I don't drop to eighty-nine pounds before my family stages an intervention. I really don't even have a lot of therapy, although I try it. What ends up happening is a combination of things: I start to get really tired of constantly freaking out about my body, I have a couple of good relationships with really supportive boyfriends, and I realize that I'm just never going to be able to be all things to all people. There's not a day when I suddenly snap out of it; I just gradually learn to like myself more. Even today, I can't say that I never have a wave of guilt after a big meal, but I'm better at putting it into perspective. And although I still have most of my "skinny clothes," I'm pretty sure I'll never wear them again.

Again: Internet message boards, and the people who populate them, are not to blame for all this. Clearly, there was—and probably still is—a significant piece of me that cared way too much about what other people thought. No matter how satisfying I found my actual work, I became obsessed with the realization that I could stretch myself beyond my limits and still come up short in the opinions of some. I've finally internalized that I have to be my own compass, to know when I'm doing as much as I can handle and weed out what's really not important.

But I feel for the young women who are venturing into this territory unaware. Who knows what triggers they have? Who can predict how they may respond to the unforeseen pressure to be perfect (whatever that means)? Will they become hypocrites, like I did, insisting that Miss America was all about the big picture while privately striving for an impossible aesthetic? I do know that I'm not alone in this experience: there are Miss Americas who have become alcoholic, anorexic, seriously depressed, even suicidal during and after their year with the crown. And I'm sure there are more than I know about—but I'll leave them to tell their own stories.

Mostly, I wonder why we have to be so mean. To me, the Internet would be best if it were governed by the same rules we follow in the rest of our lives. Go ahead with your constructive criticism; there's nothing that says we can't learn from what we read about ourselves online. But seriously, if you wouldn't stand up in a crowded room and say something loudly enough for everyone to hear, then for God's sake, don't type it into a box, leave the name blank, and press "Send." Our actions have so many consequences that can be impossible to anticipate. The Golden Rule has endured for a reason.

Sure, it might be preposterous to believe that the anonymous Web commenter genie can be stuffed back into its bottle, now that those inclined to do so have discovered a way to publicly spew vitriol without any accountability. But, hey, a girl can hope.

TWELVE

Essentially, the current era of Miss America began upon the retirement of Leonard Horn in September 1998. Not that everything changed overnight; there would be many, many incremental reinventions (both successful and unsuccessful) between that year and today. But several factors immediately began to develop that would cripple the leadership, limit the pageant's appeal, and make Miss America's year of service look more and more like Moses and company wandering in the desert.

First of all, it's critical to understand one fundamental truth. Regardless of the pageant's popularity and/or success throughout its nearly one hundred years of existence, the internal structure of the company has pretty much always been definable in one of two ways: at any given moment, it is either completely chaotic or tightly controlled. The Disorganized Mess Years most certainly began at Miss America's inception, and they continued until Lenora Slaughter exerted her iron grip on the day-to-day activities of the pageant. And the Autocratic Leader Years were marked by the bosses themselves: Slaughter's term, for sure, and the respective rules of Marks and Horn. Nearly every moment of the pageant's history fits snugly into one of these categories, with the other popping in from time to time to keep things interesting. One could argue, for example, that Miss America lapsed into a bit of a Disorganized Mess moment while the women's movement was in its heyday—back on its heels, unsure how to react, slow to adapt and re-brand itself—even though there was a strong individual leading the program at that time.

Additionally, the pageant's progress has always had one wild card: the impossible-to-predict arrival of a transformational Miss America, who pushes the organization forward with her presence, her innovative ideas, the mere force of her personality, or some combination thereof. Jean Bartel did it, Bess Myerson and Yolande Betbeze did it, Lee Meriwether did it—although mostly by timing and circumstance. Rebecca King (1974) and Tawny Godin (1976) did it, when they refused to hide their more-liberal-than-average political views at the height of second-wave feminism. Vanessa Williams did it, partly because of her racial identity and partly because at that point, all press was arguably good press. Kaye Lani Rae Rafko did it not only by turning her year into a crusade, but by accomplishing that with enough grace and passion that Horn quickly incorporated her initiatives into the institutional structure. Marjorie Vincent (1991) was the first to take on a dark and complicated platform; she repeatedly pointed out that there were (at the time) more shelters for abused animals than for abused women. Leanza Cornett shelved the crown at a time when Miss America badly needed intellectual and social legitimacy. Heather Whitestone allowed the pageant to ride the wave of societal acceptance for people with disabilities, reinforcing the commonly stated ideal that mentally or physically challenged Americans could still achieve remarkable things.

So Miss America herself, depending on her message and how well she articulated it, certainly had the ability to light up the pageant in the minds of the public and the media.

But no matter how successful she might be in this undertaking, she has always depended on an administrative structure and efficiency of execution that are completely beyond her control. In a very specific way, she remained as passive as her critics had always accused her of being: she could go out and give a barn burner of a speech, but the next day she was required to pack up her belongings, have someone else load her luggage, and go wherever she was told. It is a unique kind of autonomy, unaccompanied by actual independence. Her moments to shine were—and still are—utterly controlled by the organization's leadership of the moment, and executed by an ever-changing staff in the national office.

Since Leonard Horn's departure in 1998, there has been a curious phenomenon at work: the Miss America Organization has, more often than not, been operating in *both* the Disorganized Mess *and* the Autocratic Leader modes. Much of this, it can be argued, is specifically attributable to the evolution of the pageant's governance. Technically, the board of directors is in charge of the Miss America Organization; like most boards, they have hiring and firing power over the chief executive officer. But over the years, the executives got stronger and more savvy, while the board remained largely composed of local volunteers who were gradually given more influence. Miss America has never had a board, for example, with substantial collective ability to raise capital and solicit sponsorships. Nor has the board been made up specifically of individuals who were powerful in their respective fields. The majority of the board members, in fact, have historically been dedicated volunteers who were ultimately promoted to top-dog status. To those who spent years, even decades, giving their time as hostesses or on security detail, being asked to join the board was the ultimate compliment. Miss America was consistently the most revered event within a hundred-mile radius. Being invited to serve on the board of directors was

its own reward; it represented a social status and significance that were to be respected.

Not that the board members stopped trying. Quite the
opposite. As a body, they donated thousands of hours per
year. They organized, managed, and staged a massive
event, one that grew into a multimillion-dollar nonprofit
company. Each had his or her own specific spheres of responsibility, but not all of them were skilled at overseeing
the performance of an executive with a six-figure salary.
In fact, since many had achieved significant private-sector
success—to a degree that allows a person to make this kind
of volunteer commitment—it could be difficult for some of
them to gain perspective on the salary issues, staffing, and
operations of the tax-exempt corporation Miss America
had become.

So with a governing body made up of volunteers, most of
whom had earned their board of directors stripes through
Miss America itself, the burden of big-picture thinking and
strategy naturally shifted toward the staff side. Lenora
Slaughter was, of course, a tough Southerner determined
to bring the pageant respectability above all else. Al Marks
was an investment broker; after his thirty-five-year term
ended, he was referred to as "the Miss America Pageant's
pygmalion." And Leonard Horn, who among other things
was an extremely skilled talker, learned to work the board
votes through a combination of persuasion and strong-arm
tactics.

What this inevitably created was a board of directors
who, by and large, were accustomed to receiving updates,
instead of creating big concepts and assessing deliver-
ables. And Miss America could function like this, as long
as the right CEO was in place. The right CEO was familiar
enough with the pageant to recognize both its greatest assets and its inherent Achilles heels, along with a fairly en-
cyclopedic knowledge of what had worked—and what had
not—in the past. If the executive possessed these quali-

ties, it was possible for the board members to expend most of their energy on actually executing the annual pageant, while the staff and CEO did the work on messaging. It's a counterintuitive way for a corporation to function; most nonprofits, for example, assign the big-picture policymaking to the board of directors and the day-to-day tasks to the staff. But it can work the other way as well. There is a price, however: this approach can create a more passive and less empowered board of directors, not to mention cause the poor soul charged with conducting an institutional audit to have an aneurysm in light of the possible negative outcomes of such an arrangement.

This is not unique to Miss America, of course; CEOs have manipulated and pressured trustees and directors for . . . well, about as long as there have been CEOs, trustees, and directors. In this situation, however, very few checks and balances existed. One notable exception was the National Association of Miss America State Pageants (NAMASP), a half–support staff, half-union entity composed of high-ranking volunteers from around the country. NAMASP held regular national meetings (usually one in the first quarter of each year, and one during Miss America week in September). It provided training and support for the pageants and directors—both local and state—that were new to the program. How to raise scholarship funds. How to put on a pageant on a budget. How to position your organization within the community and solicit support and sponsorship from business owners. How to legitimately gain nonprofit status, so that donations from outside entities can be pitched to those entities as tax deductions.

But NAMASP also policed both its own members and the national MAO office. Because it actually shouldered all the man-hours and most of the expense of running the state pageants (on which the national office is completely dependent in order to have fifty-plus contestants show up at the national competition each year), it had built-in leverage. With its revolving democracy of governance—leadership positions rotated according to geographical region—NAMASP could often keep the CEO in check when the board either didn't understand the big picture or couldn't get the votes to have sufficient influence.

After all, NAMASP members, along with Miss America herself, were the ones who were actually on the scene; while the national executive could certainly have perspective on the big picture, he or she did most of the pageant's business nestled in the Miss America–loving haven of Atlantic City. Miss America was out in front of the public every day, and even the least attentive titleholder witnessed the full spectrum of reactions to both her title and the organization as a whole. But because of the logistics of her travel schedule, it was difficult for her to consistently report back to the board of directors in order for them to initiate action and changes.

NAMASP, on the other hand, found plenty of time to offer input. Its members, along with the volunteers they supervised, have always been the ones knocking on doors, making cold calls, and soliciting sponsorships from small businesses across the country. They know why a dress shop or a car dealer might sponsor a "closed" local pageant (only contestants from that town or region can compete) and might turn down an "open" local (with participation allowed from across the state, meaning that theoretically, Miss Upper Peninsula could actually live in Detroit). The volunteers are the recipients of feedback at every level: when Miss America's branding and/or identity slips, it takes the heaviest toll on the locals. At the national level, "Miss America" has always been a recognizable brand. Even at its nadir, it conjures up images of traditional family values that provide sponsorship hooks. But when the Atlantic City leadership allows the messaging to become vague, the smaller pageants suffer. It's more difficult to secure support for the tiny Miss Vermont pageant, for example, because that state doesn't have a built-in pageant obsession like Texas does. The New England states, the mountain states, and many others need strong, sellable, and substantive branding at the national level, so that they can turn around and solicit community support for their own organizations. Mississippi, California, and South Carolina, for instance, can coast somewhat on the popularity of pageants in general (and Miss America in particular), but the trickle-down effect of big-picture marketing—or its absence—can be a make-or-break factor in areas of the country without a thriving pageant culture.

Of course, NAMASP was by no means a perfect organization. Its members were prone to jockey for position within the group; even among those who should have the most faith in the judging integrity, there is a misconception that being "in good" with the national office might benefit your state contestant at the annual competition (the MAO leadership, as one might expect, does little to correct this). There were internal squabbles over power. Issues of vastly varying importance were routinely given equal weight; the same near hysteria might greet a proposed small change in the telecast as, say, an amendment to the rules for the national competition. Those who did disagree with MAO policies would often hide behind one aggressive spokesperson, despite the reality that a united front could have provided the leverage they were seeking—especially since the Miss America Organization reserves the right to revoke any volunteer's state franchise agreement at any time, for any reason. The member states radically disagreed over the ideal priorities and meaning of Miss America, prompted by the wildly diverse view of pageants in their respective regions. Factions and cliques developed often; at one point, the Southern states decided to secede. But when the members were in agreement and avoided dysfunction, NAMASP could be very powerful.

Horn notably had squabbles with NAMASP, although

THE UGLY PAGEANT

he was a good enough leader (or manipulator, depending on whom one asks) to keep the group largely in check. His speeches about transforming Miss America "from being a passive beauty queen to a motivated social activist" were generally pretty inspiring. And unlike some other executives, Horn actually listened to many of the concerns of the states. He may have believed that he had most of the answers, but he could admit when there were questions he hadn't thought of. Plus, his introduction of the platform issue gave the states something to sell to prospective supporters. When a local bookstore owner asked why she should sponsor Miss America instead of any number of other worthy organizations, the answer was far more valuable to everyone than it had been in prior years. Not only was Miss America using that money for scholarships, not only was the donation a tax write-off, but the bookstore owner should probably know that the current Miss America was dedicating her entire year to adult literacy (1997). Or school-to-work programs (1996). Or education (2001). Horn's platform issue had marketable value and credibility that the smaller scale pageants desperately needed to stay alive.

But then Leonard Horn left Miss America. It has been strongly rumored that he was pushed out, either by a board of directors that was tired of being marginalized or by the NAMASP volunteers who feared that his influence was becoming too great. Ironically, it would be the power vacuum left by his departure that would cause the pageant far greater long-term problems.

By most accounts, Horn was directly involved in the selection of his immediate successor, Rob Beck; in fact, he was on the six-member search committee that interviewed the candidates. Beck, who had headed up both Mothers Against Drunk Driving and the U.S. Soccer Federation Foundation, was intentionally chosen because he was an outsider to the pageant world. The belief among many was that the years of promoting staff from within the organization may have caused MAO to operate in a bubble. Beck's skill set met what the search committee claimed to be looking for: "a CEO with Horn's energy, leadership skills and vision. A marketing and financial background, along with good personal skills, are essential," then–board president David Frisch remarked during the search process. Additionally, Horn was reportedly "looking forward to training his replacement."

Indeed, following Beck's selection, he was a pageant-week fixture at Horn's side during the festivities. Horn was being celebrated on the way out, but he was also introducing the guy on the way in. It was a necessary stamp of approval for an executive who would soon be alone at the helm of a giant and unwieldy corporation, particularly one with which he had no previous experience. Unfortunately for Rob Beck, Leonard Horn's demonstration of support turned out to be woefully insufficient.

Beck's tenure lasted only about a year. It would end with both literal and figurative hurricanes. Floyd barreled toward the Jersey Shore during pageant week, threatening to interrupt the festivities. Union Local 54 went on strike, knocking out all housekeeping and food service at the casino hotels. And a single proposed rule change infuriated many of the volunteers, turned the pageant into a national punch line, and generated a firestorm of questionable publicity.

But in the beginning, there was a great deal of excitement about having a new face around the office. One member of the board of directors (who wished to remain anonymous due to the confidential nature of board meetings) believed that Beck showed a great deal of promise. A year, however, is hardly an abundance of time to learn the ins and outs of an institution that is almost eighty years old.

Beck seemed to fall especially short when it came to understanding the nuances of both messaging and power. Early in his term, he floated the idea of publicizing the personal financial benefit of winning the Miss America title. At the time, in addition to her scholarships, the winner's speaking fees quickly catapulted her from unknown college student into a member of the top 3 percent of American wage earners. Only a Miss America who had regularly experienced the expectations of the media and the public (those being, of course, that Miss America should probably be working for free) could argue that this was a poor idea. As the platform issue continued to occupy the front-and-center position on the list of MAO's priorities, the last thing the pageant needed was to backslide into the kind of upper-class identity that could hike Miss America back onto her pedestal. Beck, however, seemed unconvinced that this would be more of a hindrance than an asset.

He also endeavored to increase the entertainment value of the televised talent competition, by informing the state organizations that backup singers, dancers, and other production elements would be added to what the contestants had prepared. Again, in theory, it's completely plausible that his intentions were pure, and that he was just doing a little good old-fashioned outside-the-box thinking. It's also staggeringly obvious that he had little to no grasp of the impact that these last-minute changes would likely have on the actual young women who were competing for Miss America. Although there are certainly some contestants whose stated career ambitions involve the entertainment industry—and a significantly smaller percentage who ever really make a living wage in show business—there are many, many more who haven't taken dance classes since they went off to college, or who learn one song to sing at every pageant. To add last-minute "support" performers into a Broadway show is not a big deal; to try it with these non-professional artists (already under a great deal of pageant week stress) would almost definitely have caused chaos, anguish, and enough tears to sink a cruise ship. And from a judging standpoint, it would have been an unnecessary distraction—especially if, say, a rogue backup dancer decided that the national TV exposure was a valid reason to pull focus.

This kind of thinking may have been symptomatic of what was to come in Beck's term. As the first non-insider CEO since Al Marks began to grab the reins in 1952, his tenure illuminated that Miss America involves many nuances which are invisible to the inexperienced eye. But it was the kind of thing that any thinking person (which Beck undoubtedly was and is) could have learned over time. Although at least one board member would later publicly criticize Beck's management style, there really aren't many examples indicating that he had personality issues that caused clashes, especially as compared to Horn, or to some of the men who would succeed him in the CEO position. Ultimately, Rob Beck's greatest transgression was trying to change too much, too fast, in an organization that would quickly demonstrate that it was seriously allergic to change.

Several months into his term, Beck began reviewing the Miss America contestant contract, with the help of pageant attorney Steven Perskie. The two men had an eye toward revising the document as a whole, rather than in the piecemeal fashion in which it had previously been amended. Perskie—who later became a Superior Court judge—reportedly became especially concerned about some of the New Jersey discrimination laws the pageant might run up against if a situation ever arose that required enforcement of certain clauses.

What hastened Beck's departure, of course, was not a mere review of the contract, or his desire to avoid discrimination against potential contestants. It was that his proposed rule change would no longer prohibit women who had been married or pregnant from entering the Miss America program. On its surface, the concept had merit: the Miss America Organization could have conceivably been confronted, at any time, with a legal battle from a potential contestant who had given birth after being a victim of rape or incest. In fact, MAO would soon face—and amicably resolve—a challenge from a sexually abused young woman in Oklahoma who had become pregnant, and ultimately had given the baby up for adoption. But Beck didn't yet have that situation as ammunition to propel his initiative. When the press picked up the story, it was quickly and irrevocably framed as a move to allow divorced women and those who had had abortions to become Miss America.

With that kind of damage threatening the Miss America brand—the program that the volunteers had to sell to potential small-town sponsors as one that selected a role model for the nation each year—NAMASP sprang into action. In 1999 (while that year's contestants were actually in Atlantic City, no less), they sued the pageant to block the rule change. Although Beck agreed to hold off on implementation for a year, the national media had picked up on the story. It made headlines across the country, and the Miss America Organization became "prime fodder for late night comedians" as a result. Beck was fired two weeks after the crowning of the new Miss America.

Beck filed a wrongful-termination lawsuit against the Miss America board of directors. In it, he claimed that he was fired without just cause. There was one more juicy detail in the case; his lawsuit accused Leonard Horn of colluding with board members to push him out of his job. Attorneys claimed that "the former CEO continued to hold sway over at least some members of the national board of directors and was instrumental in getting Beck fired . . . they sought to add Horn to the list of defendants because of 'tortious interference with the contractual relationship of plaintiff (Beck) and his employer, the Miss America Or-

ganization.'" Although numerous board members were de-
posed, and Horn's letter to Beck (in which he told his replacement that he "should be ashamed" of himself) was
admitted as part of the court record, Horn never legally became a defendant in the case. It was ultimately resolved
in 2003, when a New Jersey judge reportedly awarded
Beck $80,000 in severance pay. But his problematic ten-
ure, which wreaked havoc on all involved parties—and,
more critically, on Miss America's public image—had more
than one lesson to offer those who would try to lead the organization in the future. To some extent, it was likely that
Leonard Horn was still involved behind the scenes, and un-
interested in allowing new leadership to dilute his legacy.
Additionally, NAMASP was not to be trifled with, and was
not afraid to air Miss America's dirty laundry in the press,
if an executive was threatening what NAMASP considered
to be a cornerstone of its institution. This detail, in particular, would be an essential one for the pageant in the coming years.

With Rob Beck's time as CEO over, the pageant moved
quickly to select his successor; the pressure to put
on an annual telecast doesn't allow a lot of time for leadership squabbles or power vacuums. This time, the board
stuck a little closer to home. In February 2000, they announced that they had found their man.

As the new head honcho, MAO chose Robert Renneisen,
a Vietnam veteran with a journalism degree. Most recently,
Renneisen had spent several years as CEO of Claridge Casino and Hotel. (That the Claridge declared bankruptcy
around the same time they let him go was, apparently, not
a deal breaker for the pageant. In hindsight, it probably
should have been.)

Renneisen was a smooth operator: handsome, charming,
the owner of a great sense of humor. He also had the confi-

dence that came with having saved an Atlantic City institution from financial ruin; along with a section of Resorts International, the Claridge is still the only original hotel on the Boardwalk that hasn't been demolished to make way for a shiny new casino.

The new boss had also apparently learned quite a bit from the very public fiasco of the preceding year. Almost immediately, he reassured the pageant faithful that he had only the best intentions regarding their sparkly, glamorous baby. He compared Miss America to cultural icons like the Washington Monument, and dismissed questions about revisiting the controversial contractual clauses that had gotten Rob Beck fired.

Renneisen also expressed a desire to substantially grow the pageant's financial stability, in terms of both sponsorship and scholarship. What might have seemed like empty ambition from someone else seemed attainable for this CEO; Renneisen had rescued the Claridge from debt a few years earlier, to the tune of about $85 million. And he seemed deeply committed to the mission of the pageant, stating at the time that "if I can get five minutes with a senior educator or senior corporate executive, only five minutes so I can explain what this program does, their perceptions can be changed forever."

It didn't take him long to get started. By the fall, he had planned and initiated a "Five Minutes With Miss America" tour. Accompanied by the newly crowned Angela Perez Baraquio (2001), Renneisen logged plenty of miles courting potential corporate partners for Miss America, as well as attempting to dispel stereotypes about the organization. Although it was an interesting big-picture idea, the campaign was met with skepticism in some quarters. Perhaps as a result of insufficient advance work from the pageant office, the press seemed as interested in what Baraquio ate in those five minutes as in what she said. Some reporters implied that the pageant's central message—and mission—

was confusing and conflicted. "For years, Miss America has dressed in swimsuits and then complained that Miss America is more than dressing in swimsuits," noted the *San Francisco Chronicle*, adding that "her appearances are preceded by a pleading letter from her Miss America handlers." Clearly, the new boss's team had underestimated the scope of the task they were confronting, as well as the difficulty of raising capital for a nonprofit scholarship organization versus a revenue-producing casino hotel.

Meanwhile, Renneisen also set about reinventing Miss America from the inside out. The stubbornly mom-and-pop vibe of the organization was likely frustrating to him, especially when it served as a deterrent to the big business he was trying to attract. In what was presumably an effort to bring the pageant into the twenty-first century, he went on a hiring spree, adding several vice presidents to the payroll—some of whom were promoted from within, while some came from the business world; one was even a former volunteer state pageant director. Over a period of several months, the staff grew to include an executive vice president, a senior vice president of marketing, a director of field operations, and a public relations manager. Of course, so many new six-figure salaries also guaranteed that Miss America's operating expenses would balloon. And they did, initiating a disturbing financial trend. In 2000, total functional expenses were $3,994,722, against $10,289,792 in assets and $2,923,238 in revenue. By 2002, however, it was reported that the pageant had "plunged $1 million into the red" and operating expenses had pushed the organization to the brink of insolvency. Never shy about chiming in, Leonard Horn continued to be at the top of the list when journalists needed quotes for their stories. He publicly complained about the whittling down of the $10 million reserve he had left behind, claiming that "the money that the pageant had is being thrown away."

Like his predecessors, Renneisen looked to move the

pageant forward. But once again, repos
zation of MAO's size and structure turt   tic
ficult job. His term—which lasted bare   R
marked by choices widely criticized by M   te
work of volunteers and unflatteringly fr   gi
dia. To his credit, Renneisen did take bold   A
to reinvent the pageant's image and sho   h
tion up financially. But unlike Rob Beck, 1   t
able moves could be explained by a general   c
zational experience and savvy, Renneisen h
the pageant for a while. And as a former head
sino, he certainly knew the ins and outs of
dealings. It's difficult, therefore, to see how 1
failed to anticipate the surprise, and even h
would greet some of his more memorable initia

Like licensing a Miss America slot machit
objective standpoint, this may have seemed
brainer; at that point, Atlantic City had been a c
for two decades. The problem, though, is clear
with a deeper understanding of Miss America's
ship with its hometown: for most of those year,
tants were expressly forbidden to even set foot on
ing floor in their pageant week host hotels. Even i
rules loosened in the late 1990s, one was about as .
see a saltwater taffy ban on the Boardwalk as to 1
any Miss State gambling in early September—at lei
til after the Saturday-night finals, after which all b
customarily off, so to speak. It's not that Miss Americ
and officials find gambling inherently distasteful; ple
them spend time in the casinos when they're not occt
by preliminary competitions. But Miss America is not
posed to be like other mortals. And as incongruous as
for many fans to imagine their favorite hopeful striving
triple 7's instead of getting her beauty sleep and exercisi
it is altogether unconscionable that she might be trying
hit triple Phyllis Georges.

In addition to underestimating contemporary ramifications of the pageant's deeply conservative moral tradition, Renneisen made it known that he was willing to slaughter another sacred cow: unless Atlantic City stepped up its game, he hinted, he might move Miss America elsewhere. Again, his trademark confidence and local experience may have bolstered him in this decision; in order even to raise the question of whether the pageant should stay or go, one would want to have a few trump cards firmly in one's pocket. In response to Renneisen's threat, a task force was formed to discuss the additional $1 million he had insisted was necessary to keep Miss America from packing up her crown and scepter . . . most likely bound for the Mohegan Sun Casino in Connecticut. The fallout was problematic, and ultimately the pageant did not get the requested funding.

In the end, though, Bob Renneisen was handed his walking papers (the official statement was that he quit, but it was obvious that he did so under enormous pressure) by the same entity that had sounded the death knell for Rob Beck: the National Association of Miss America State Pageants.

In early February 2002, a letter from the parents of Katie Harman (2002) was leaked to the press. The question of how exactly this happened elicited plenty of conflicting answers. The *New York Times* reported that the state pageant organizations had circulated it. Later, *Salon's* Jake Tapper reported that it had actually been Renneisen himself, presumably making a power play. In any case, the eight-page document was damning, with allegations that Harman was being mistreated by pageant officials.

"Katie is your Miss America and I can't tell you how many times she is 'in trouble' for things that are not her fault," read the letter from Darla Harman to the MAO board of directors. Apparently, Harman was repeatedly being charged for some significant job-related expenses . . . items that had historically been underwritten by the or-

ganization. Some were small, like clothing alterations, but the MAO staff had also sent her an invoice for $2,248 for her own post-crowning party at the Trump Taj Mahal.

Renneisen believed that the letter was part of a plot to oust him from power. Frustrated by trying to reconcile the organization's need to evolve and the will of its critical volunteer network, he had thrown down the gauntlet at NAMASP's January meeting. When confronted by the concerns of state directors who felt that MAO was not running efficiently, he advised them to "'get the hell out' of the Miss America Organization and then abruptly left the meeting."

Renneisen's strategy—take an aggressive stance, refuse to let the states run the show—was bold, but not unprecedented. However, he significantly underestimated the will and influence of the longtime volunteers. Again, without them, there *was* no Miss America Pageant in September; there simply wasn't time (not to mention funding) to outsource the work of running hundreds of local pageants and fifty-one state pageants each year. Like many new leaders, Renneisen had been amiable at first, saying the right things about wanting input and collaboration. Ultimately, though, his leadership style turned out to be vertical. And while vertical leadership can be effective, it certainly doesn't work if it's masquerading as horizontal leadership. "In the history of Miss America, I can't ever recall this level of anger. These people don't normally do these things. They don't go to the press. They normally suffer in silence," Leonard Horn mused at the time.

Finally, there was one more thing that must have completely blindsided Renneisen. No matter what relationships he felt he had cultivated with both the pageant community and the Atlantic City decision makers, those connections paled in comparison with the years, even decades, that NAMASP members had spent with the board of directors. Although NAMASP and the pageant board were, of course, two separate organizations, they united every year in the service of a common cause. Because of the composition of the board (the head of security, the head of the Hostess Committee, etc.), there was a lot of shared territory. After all, NAMASP members did basically the same thing back home in their states that the MAO board did each September in Atlantic City. Renneisen might have survived the storm if he had had a board of directors made up of powerful businesspeople or heavy-hitting fund-raisers. But he didn't. He had a group of people who had been doing all the work of putting on the pageant, some of them for decades, for free. The board members were far more likely to relate to the longtime volunteers than to some hotshot businessman who wanted to tell everybody what to do—even though, of course, they had selected and hired him for precisely that purpose. And, of course, it didn't help Renneisen's cause that the Miss America board has never been known for its commitment to confidentiality. Pageants are a gossipy business to begin with, and old habits are hard to break.

Four state pageant directors went to the swanky new Atlantic City offices on February 4, 2002, met with Bob Renneisen, and requested his resignation. Sometime after that, Glen and Darla Harman's letter went public. A media circus ensued. MAO staff began to cancel Harman's upcoming appearances, letting her cool her heels in a Des Moines hotel while they tried to figure out what to do. Ultimately, the decision was made to bring her back to Atlantic City for a dog-and-pony press conference.

Harman was told that according to the terms of her contract, she was obligated to defend the Miss America Organization. It was implied that she could be fired if she didn't stand in front of the assembled media and essentially call her parents liars. From the outside, it seems preposterous that this would actually happen. But despite her maturity and poise, Harman was just twenty-one at the time. The brutal schedule that Miss Americas must maintain cuts them off from their support systems: friends, parents, and certainly any lawyers in the family. Most of all, the majority of Miss America contestants are people-pleasers. The implication that Harman was ungrateful, lacked humility, or was otherwise behaving like a diva would have worked to push her down the path of least resistance. And the threat of being forced out as Miss America would have been devastating.

So, on February 15, a tearful Miss America went through with the press conference. At the time, rumors circulated that Renneisen was poised to accuse Darla Harman of having an undisclosed mental illness if her daughter didn't comply with his marching orders. But although the press reported that fences had been mended, the internal tension only got worse. In the minds of many, the CEO had committed two inexcusable acts. First, he had piled the organization's leadership problems onto a very well-liked Miss America, whose first appearances had included visiting the rescue workers at the still-smoldering World Trade Center. And second, he had done the unthinkable by openly exhibiting the extent of his contempt for NAMASP and its members, calling their list of grievances—many of which were legitimate—"the rebellion of the beauty queens." At the time, he complained that "this organization is staffed throughout the country by people who are predominantly volunteers . . . some of whom, frankly, have no other life than this. They have collected 12 years of petty gripes and groans and are trying to put it all in Katie's mouth."

Two weeks later, Bob Renneisen was out as the CEO of the Miss America Organization.

After blowing through two CEOs in three years, it seems the board decided to devote some time to considering how to fill the position. By this point, it was clear that managing the Miss America Organization was trickier than most had expected. In many respects, it was still a mom-and-pop enterprise. But the often-conflicting demands of the media, the volunteer network, and the pageant's financial situation resulted in something of a mess. Frank Deford, whose insights had typically been spot-on regarding the MAO, was blunt about the "turmoil" he observed within the pageant. "Miss America can't decide who it is and what it wants to be. Until it does, these kind of problems are going to continue." Atlantic City historian Vicki Gold Levi wondered if any CEO without significant pageant experience would be able to balance the competing interests of the "many masters" the executive was obligated to please.

Although most of the mainstream media had gradually tuned out the pageant over the preceding years, the abundance of controversy coaxed plenty of writers to take another look. Even the hometown paper was losing faith; an op-ed piece in the *Press of Atlantic City* presented more questions than answers:

Why is a relatively simple enterprise such as a nonprofit beauty (OK, "scholarship") pageant so often the subject of so much controversy?

Consider just recent events: There are secrets—financial books that no one will open, whispers about extravagant spending and unnecessary hires.

There are the state pageant officials who recently came to Atlantic City to complain about a climate of "fear and intimidation."

There is that letter that the parents of Miss America 2002 Katie Harman wrote to complain that they and their daughter are mistreated by the pageant organization (and Miss America 1998 Kate Shindle piping up in support of Harman's parents).

And then . . . almost like some POW making a forced statement . . . there is Harman herself, trotted out at a press conference to say, more or less, golly gee it's all a mistake and everything is just hunky-dory as far as she's concerned.

Why is the Miss America Organization not a modern, transparent enterprise that is run openly, professionally, and peacefully?

One positive outcome of Renneisen's hiring spree: although he had wreaked havoc on the pageant's finances, he had unwittingly created a pool of candidates to succeed him in the position. As interim CEO, the board appointed vice president George Bauer, a fifty-eight-year-old former international businessman who had been Renneisen's right-hand man. Bauer didn't have the same easy charm as his predecessor, but he had a pronounced tan that never seemed to fade, extremely white teeth, and a reputation for being something of a ladies' man. At the time, there were rumors that Renneisen and Bauer, who had at one point been very close friends, had had a falling-out during their time together at MAO. After his departure, Renneisen began studying to become a priest.

Like Renneisen before him, Bauer immediately expressed his intent to bridge the troubled waters separating the volunteers and the paid staff. "I don't think we want to rule over 51 (state) people. We want to work with 51 people. There is a lot of experience out there, and I'm going to tap into it," he said.

He also faced serious challenges regarding the pageant's financial situation. At that point, things were beginning to look pretty dire; the state organizations wanted to know if the proposed move out of Atlantic City was a signal that he was having trouble securing new sponsorships. Somewhat lost in the shuffle over the preceding weeks was a story that provided a clue as to why old sponsors were departing and new ones weren't exactly lining up in the hallway outside the corner office. The pageant had reportedly

shown little respect for—and even less ability to collaborate with—some of the vendors whose services they used
each year. Most outspoken was Joseph J. Trefaller of Pic-
cari Press, the longtime publisher of Miss America's program book. His company had "offered $250,000 in corpo-
rate subsidies over a five-year period—on the condition
of 'a complete change of the executive/management staff
of the Miss America Organization.'" The company's vice
president, Harry Eaby, added, "Thank goodness there are
51 state organizations who woke up and realized there's
something really wrong in Atlantic City." Eaby asserted
that "the pageant has little knowledge of basic marketing
practices and refused to return phone calls to both contractors and major sponsors."

In fact, there was growing distrust of both the board and
the staff, even among those in Atlantic City and surround-
ing environs who were involved with the pageant. Part of
this is attributable to the fact that the Jersey Shore con-
sists of a series of small towns. They bustle in the summer,
but the community of people who live there year-round is
relatively modest in size. And the full-time residents are
much more likely to have skin in the Miss America game.
The Hostess Committee, for example, actually established
a geographical boundary beyond which no hostess could
live. Being a hostess was a year-round commitment involv-
ing fund-raisers and other events, not just shuttling the
contestants back and forth to rehearsals. If you weren't local, you were out of luck. But once you made it into the club,
it was likely that you developed strong relationships with
your fellow volunteers—and probably plenty of opinions
about how things were going. For a volunteer entrenched
in the Miss America culture, the threat that Miss America might relocate would be devastating. And for those politicians, personalities, and merchants who were invested
in the pageant, the exploration of other venues—*especially*

other casino venues—came across as enormously disloyal. This led to what Bob Renneisen had called an "intolerable" attitude toward the organization, specifically noting that "members of the pageant's board have received tremendous animosity from the public and had their motives questioned."

In reality, what had seemed like a betrayal to Renneisen may have looked more like fiscal responsibility to his Atlantic City colleagues. The mayor at the time, James Whelan, who began his pageant affiliation as a lifeguard volunteering at the Miss America parade and became a reliable supporter, wondered publicly if the pageant was providing enough value for the dollars the city was spending to keep it. Around the same time, Freeholder James Carney was "questioning the Miss America Organization's ability to manage the pageant's finances," adding in a letter to the board, "You may have lost your focus on the real goal of the Miss America Organization of providing scholarship money to young women. Possibly a better handle on expenses could help make up your deficit." He went on to state that there were those who felt a shakedown was happening, as the pageant tried to secure more financial backing.

Finally, there was still the matter of whether the current board of directors would ever be able to rise to the challenge of actually leading the organization, of guiding its executive rather than being guided by him. While the board had issued few public statements during the preceding weeks, the ones that made it into print weren't all that encouraging. On February 15, the day of Katie Harman's coerced press conference, the board still apparently didn't see what the big fuss was all about. Board member David Sparenberg took a direct, irrelevant, and rather cheap swipe at Rob Beck, saying that "unlike his predecessor, Bob is not autocratic," and went on to state that he and his colleagues were "very satisfied" with the job he was doing.

If nothing else, Miss America's troubles during this era were consistent. For Bauer, the substantial challenges began in July 2002 when the new Miss North Carolina, Rebekah Revels, abruptly resigned shortly after being crowned. The situation would culminate in a public relations nightmare that prompted the *Chicago Tribune* to label the organization "hypocritical and cowardly," after the press got wind that Revels had been forced out. "Revels was pressured to resign the crown because a guy she now claims abused her as a teenager crawled out from underneath his rock in late July and fired off an e-mail to Miss America Organization officials. The gist of it read, 'Ask her about the two nude photos.'" Revels recounted a situation in which her former flame sneaked a couple of photos while she was getting dressed. But state officials allegedly convinced her that the existence of the photos violated the contract's vague morals clause. The *Tribune* story continued:

> Although [national pageant] officials apparently never saw the photos in question and never spoke directly with Revels, they sent word that she had no shot at Miss America's crown.
>
> Given that she would effectively be knocking her home state out of contention for the title if she participated, Revels decided to take one for the team and resign.
>
> George Bauer, interim president of the organization, issued the following disingenuous statement on July 26:
>
> "Although the Miss America Organization regrets the circumstances surrounding Rebekah Revels' previous relationship with her former fiance and is concerned for her well-being, it was she who voluntarily chose to resign her position as Miss North Carolina 2002."

Apparently, though, Revels's decision wasn't really all that voluntary. Writing at the time for *Salon,* Jake Tapper recounted that she soon decided to bring a lawsuit against the pageant, claiming that she had been forced out—and that she should still get to compete in Atlantic City in September. A Raleigh judge reinstated her. When both Revels and her first runner-up, Misty Clymer (who had been appointed when Revels stepped down) showed up for the national pageant, there were two Miss North Carolinas in Atlantic City. Revels must have felt unwelcome, but she surged ahead with her effort to participate, even signing the giant map that each contestant autographs on arrival day. Revels's inscription on the Tar Heel State? "The Forget Me Not Campaign." The circus continued for several days; Tapper characterized their eventual joint Boardwalk press conference as "Begin-and-Sadat style."

Revels lost the battle shortly before the start of preliminary competition, when District Court Judge James Fox declined to force the Miss America Organization to recognize Revels as a contestant. Almost as soon as the words were out of his mouth, the pageant essentially kicked Revels to the curb in favor of Misty Clymer.

Clymer made the top ten. Revels was invited to stay as a VIP guest and watch the competition. She did, however, continue to pursue litigation back home. Although Judge Fox declined to extend Revels's injunction to keep the pageant from happening without her, he did not rule on several other issues. Revels contended that although she had not participated in the Miss America Pageant, she had still been reinstated in North Carolina. Ultimately, her lawsuit against Miss America dragged on until 2007, when "the state Court of Appeals rejected her claims that she was illegally barred from taking part in the 2002 national pageant." However, as a result of the litigation, the Miss North Carolina Pageant recognizes neither Revels nor Clymer. No doubt reflecting the desire of many to forget the whole mess, it simply skips the year 2002 in the parade of former titleholders on its website.

Shortly thereafter, Bauer encountered another big headache: some serious difficulties with "his" first Miss America, Erika Harold (2003). Harold had competed several times before winning the Miss Illinois title. Her ultra-conservative views had proven to be a bit too extreme for some judges; one year, she had failed to make the top ten after her answer to a question about same-sex adoption in her private interview: under pressure, Harold reportedly stated that she would choose to place a child in an abusive heterosexual home rather than with a loving gay couple. Unfortunately for her, one of her judges had recently adopted a child with his longtime partner. Another told friends that because of that single answer, he had dropped her interview score from a 10 to 2. Although judges are trained not to score contestants directly on their personal or political values, they are instructed to evaluate the young woman's ability to state her opinions in a diplomatic and appropriate manner. Like everyone, pageant contestants say plenty of things that they think better of later. But if a winner publicly flubbed an answer as badly as Harold did privately, the fallout would be disastrous. If a young woman can't find a way to mitigate her more polarizing views, she identifies herself as a potential loose cannon and pretty much disqualifies herself from getting the job.

Harold then took a year off from competing, grew up a bit, and came back like gangbusters. She won the Miss Illinois title with a combination of intelligence, tenacity, and academic credentials; she was a stellar student and had been accepted to what were then "the country's five leading law schools," ultimately deciding on Harvard.

A relevant detail: 2002 was the first year that the Miss Illinois Pageant had adopted a statewide platform issue that would replace the contestant's own platform issue. Realistically, it's difficult for a state organization to start from scratch every year. With the anti-bullying program that was created that year, each new winner would build upon the work of the previous titleholders, and allow the state organization to foster lasting relationships with non-profits, legislators, and sponsors. But although Harold—like all of the contestants—signed the contract stipulating this along with the other particulars of the job, she apparently wasn't thrilled about it. Her own platform issue, advocating for abstinence-only sex education programs, was a longtime passion of hers. She had served as a youth advocate since age eighteen; in fact, "by the time she won Miss Illinois . . . Erika had addressed 14,000 youth in Illinois schools about making proper sexual decisions." This work had ushered her into social and political circles with prominent figures like NFL Hall of Famer Mike Singletary and especially longtime conservative activist Phyllis Schlafly, who could potentially be future assets to her stated plans to run for public office.

Despite some reported grumbling, Harold did indeed go to Atlantic City with anti-bullying initiatives as her platform. As it turned out, she had been aggressively targeted by other students during her early years; her personal story included compelling details about her time growing up. "She was called a whore, she said. Her home was vandalized by bullies. Fellow ninth-graders even pooled money to buy a gun and kill her." Bolstered again by her potential to be a game-changing Miss America—in part because a Miss America who had already been accepted to Harvard Law would undoubtedly generate a great deal of media attention—Harold swept to victory. At the time, awards for private interview and evening gown were given alongside the traditional preliminary swimsuit and talent prizes; Harold took both the private and onstage interview competitions, which presumably balanced out her unique, non-pageant brand of physical beauty.

But once she had the crown, things shifted a bit. First of all, she arrived in Atlantic City ready to start her job immediately, with national and international organizations standing by to put her right to work on their behalf. Although she did attend the "summit" she had pre-organized for her post-crowning week, the Miss America leadership was reportedly not eager for the new winner to continue those relationships. Understandably a bit paranoid about the influence of the state directors, George Bauer dismissed Harold's contacts and initiatives as "state stuff." To put it mildly, the national office—which has somehow repeatedly failed to learn the value of returning phone calls, even in the best of times—did not follow through on the opportunities that Harold brought along with her. It is the perfect example of a moment when power squabbles triumph over opportunity and common sense, and result in a huge step backward for the platform issue and its value. Sure, the platform had remained dominant for a couple of years after Leonard Horn's departure. Both Nicole Johnson (1999) and Heather French (2000) had spent their Miss America years primarily working on platform initiatives (although French had to kick and scream a bit after being advised by MAO staff that she should change her platform because there supposedly wasn't any money to be made advocating for military veterans). But Baraquio's year (2001) was a scramble for sponsorship, with less of a focus on her platform issue, character education. And Harman (2002), whose advocacy dealt with caring for terminally ill breast cancer patients, saw her work overshadowed first by 9/11— to which she quickly and enthusiastically adapted—and then by the behind-the-scenes Miss America circus. By 2003, the pageant needed an articulate, passionate, ready-made winner who could kick-start the platform issue again. The Miss America Organization desperately needed to remind the public that the pageant still had substantive value and that, at its best, it could be a training ground for the next generation of female leaders. And miracle of miracles, the MAO execs got exactly what they needed . . . but to say that they didn't take advantage of that opportunity is a gigantic understatement.

Presumably frustrated by the lack of action, Harold turned her attention to her abstinence initiative. She was smart enough to use the media to ignite her pet project. During an event at the National Press Club, writer George Archibald of the conservative *Washington Times* asked about her abstinence work. What happened next made national news for several days, as Harold asserted that she was "being muzzled."

When Miss America staff reminded her that she was contractually obligated to stick with her stated platform, instructing her to set aside the abstinence issue, Harold spun it like a seasoned pro. Her most-reported quote, "I will not be bullied," positioned MAO as a schoolyard aggressor and her as the innocent victim. Conservative groups across the country rallied behind her, as did plenty of legislators; "38 members of Congress immediately sent Harold a letter encouraging her to 'stand up for your beliefs and promote the healthy message of abstinence until marriage.'"

George Bauer was trapped. He'd used the standard MAO tactics—guilt, isolation, passive aggression, and, finally, a line drawn in the sand—and he'd been outfoxed by a twenty-two-year-old. She had been kept in check as Miss Illinois, and was ultimately required to abide by her contract. But she had cracked the code by the time she became Miss America. Not only that, but she retained a lawyer, presumably to keep from being pushed around by MAO's many unwritten credos regarding deference and obedience; none of these little customs are included in the actual signed employment contract, but they are reinforced by everything from "helpful hints" to outright pressure. She couldn't slip out of her contractual obligations entirely, but she could stick to the letter of the law while maximizing the bright light she shone on things she wanted the media to notice. It didn't serve her to let the focus settle on the fact that she had pulled a bait and switch on her employers, the organizations that had supported her, and of course her Miss America judges—at least one of whom, who championed her during and after the pageant, has privately stated that she would not have won if she had brought an abstinence platform to the national competition. (On the record, a judge did later speak about Harold's private interview: "'I never asked her about abstinence because it was never mentioned on her very, very wordy fact sheet,' says Jim Jones, a longtime AIDS activist. 'She went out of her way to hide any information about abstinence.'")

It's one thing to be a local titleholder and talk about the reasoning behind your own life choices. It's entirely another thing to throw the full weight of an eighty-year-old institution behind a young woman who endorses an educational approach that has been proven (and re-proven, and re-proven) to be utterly ineffective. But by sowing the seeds of partisan frustration, Harold was also able to maneuver around that inconvenient detail. She essentially pointed to the other side of the aisle—Miss Americas who had been permitted to advocate for comprehensive sex education and other types of controversial HIV/AIDS prevention. In reality, Harold, too, would have been allowed to take pretty much any position on issues that were directly relevant to the platform she had officially brought to the competition. But she expertly turned a contractual dispute into a scenario in which her freedom of speech was in jeopardy and her conservative values persecuted. And she quickly figured out how to frame the issue so that it seemed to fit right in with her anti-bullying initiative. She even crafted a message about the relationship between teen sexual activity and youth violence, identifying abstinence as a cure for both.

Having been so thoroughly outsmarted, Bauer had no choice but to back down. Within two days, he did. Harold would get to integrate her abstinence message into her anti-bullying initiative.

Ultimately, the Erika Harold episode was neatly and presciently summed up well before it happened, in Tapper's *Salon* piece: "After being browbeat by feminists and media elites for years, the pageant created a method of scoring that paved the way for a winner who isn't necessarily the average frat boy's choice for a roll in the hay, but who may very well end up his boss. And that woman is Erika Harold."

Tapper certainly couldn't foresee that Harold would become, in essence, the boss of her own boss, George Bauer. But in a way, it was inevitable that it would come to this. For more than a decade, MAO had rewarded young women for speaking their minds, both politically and with respect to their platform issues. The crown had elevated Miss America to the point where she had a voice. And this was the first time a Miss America had clearly and cannily used that voice to take the lead and put the organization in its place. It was the most glaring example of a phenomenon unique to Miss America in the late 1990s and early 2000s: once yesterday's demure pageant contestant evolved into today's strong and opinionated young leader, the MAO leadership had absolutely no idea what to do with her.

Clearly, George Bauer was losing control. He had lost control of the Rebekah Revels situation. He had lost control of Erika Harold. He had provided an all-access pass to *USA Today*'s Olivia Barker, who spent pageant week alongside the contestants; she actually participated in almost every phase of competition as the "52nd contestant." In return, she wrote a generally unflattering piece about the pageant, which was mostly overshadowed by all the other dovetailing PR disasters. In September 2003, Harold would pass her crown to another tough cookie, Ericka Dunlap (2004), whose platform issue of promoting cultural diversity was the manifestation of a strong African

American identity. Later, pageant officials would whisper that the two Eri(c)kas had nearly killed the pageant. It's true that they made things more difficult for the leadership, who chose a strategy that was the exact opposite of effective. Trying to quash Harold and Dunlap, or any other Miss America, was a bad idea. It would have been far smarter to try working with them, collaborating, listening to their thoughts, and allowing them to help build a better MAO. But although Miss America herself had evolved, the pageant was still hanging on to the antiquated notion that a strong woman must be controlled. It probably was no coincidence that perceived "manageability" began to pop up in Miss America judging literature and training as one of the critical personality traits for a winner.

Perhaps unsurprisingly, this was the exact moment at which the platform issue began to fade. For Bauer, it must have served as a nasty reminder to him of getting pies in the face from all directions. It did have a prominent last gasp, when Lauren Nelson (2007) became involved in a sting operation for Internet sex predators. Despite the debatable legality of this type of undertaking, the media were largely positive about Miss America posing as an underage girl to catch child molesters on Long Island. But when prosecutors called to let Nelson's scheduling manager know when she would be needed in court, they were told that her packed calendar might render her unavailable to testify. To say the least, the subsequent fallout reversed all of the positive press MAO had initially gotten.

A final note on the significance of the Rebekah Revels incident: aside from inciting a five-year legal battle of indeterminate expense, the mess pointed up that there was little coordination between the national MAO office and its state franchisees. There is no clear policy on how to handle explosive situations. MAO typically lets the states handle what they consider to be "state business," despite the fact that said state business can blow up in the face of the national pageant. This has happened again and again, when state pageants have belatedly discovered their titleholder faked her academic credentials (Ohio 1998, for example), or contestants struggle to collect the scholarships they've won (South Carolina 2002, 2004, New York 2004, California 2003, Maryland 2004, 2006, and plenty of others), or state leaders encourage contestants to write letters of support to a former executive director around the time he is sentenced to fourteen years in prison for child molestation (South Carolina again, in a little-reported doozy), or are investigated by the attorney general for tax evasion (South Carolina, for the trifecta). A 2007 *New York Times* article detailed the stories of contestants nationwide, who "describe a Miss America system in which local pageant directors do not return telephone calls and e-mail messages for months, local competitions close down before scholarships are distributed, and the fine print in contracts creates hurdles. Local winners across the country have threatened legal action, and some have taken it."

However, until the situation in question becomes a full-fledged PR disaster (and sometimes, even after it does), MAO's common practice is to stick the "state business" label on it and send it back to the state to fix. Consider one more situation that arose in South Carolina in 2010. Carl Chu, a Kansas City pageant coach, was invited to judge the Palmetto State's annual pageant. First problem? According to Miss America's own policy, coaches—and others who may benefit financially from a pageant—are prohibited from judging any competition, due to potential conflicts of interest. MAO officials should not have allowed Chu to serve as a judge, especially since at the time they were reviewing the state judging rosters very carefully. And the South Carolina leadership, who certainly knew about the rule, should also have realized that he couldn't judge. Chu himself was probably the least culpable participant in the matter; he was primarily involved in pageant systems other than Miss America, so he may not have been tracking every rule. But the state pulled a fast one, and MAO—which, for years, consistently seemed to have a palmetto-shaped blind spot—didn't provide the appropriate oversight.

Imagine the surprise, then, when Chu went public within days of the new Miss South Carolina's crowning, alleging that some very sketchy goings-on had occurred. Unlike most whistle-blowers in the Miss America rank and file, Chu didn't air his grievances anonymously in an Internet forum, or write a strongly worded letter to Atlantic City, or simply take his ball and go home pouting. And he didn't make insinuations: he flat out stated that the Miss South Carolina Pageant had been fixed.

Chu's story was unique in its directness, to be sure, but also revelatory regarding the hubris with which some state directors operated.

According to Chu, the Miss South Carolina organization's president, Joseph P. Sanders III—who, along with his wife, Gail Sanders, had run the pageant for more than fifty years and had been honored with MAO's volunteer of the year award—had not been happy with the judges' scoring of the preliminary competitions. Almost every state holds a post-preliminary meeting at which judges determine the top ten (or fifteen, in some larger states and the national finals). Although the methods change periodically, the rules about who is permitted to speak, and who is absolutely not allowed to, are consistent and very specific. Judges are allowed to speak, with time and content restrictions; the purpose is for each judge to indicate the reasons why he or she believes each of the highest-scoring contestants is (or is not) a strong candidate for the job. Directors and other officers of the pageant, however, are not allowed to participate in this conversation except to moderate the judges' discussion or to be available in the rare case when a procedural clarification needs to be made.

Sanders, however, reportedly jumped right into the fray without hesitation. In a later interview with the *Spartanburg Herald Journal*, Chu alleged that Sanders reprimanded the judges for the quality of their scoring. And it didn't stop there; Sanders allegedly "lobbied on several contestants' behalf, [and] brought up several of the girls' family histories and wealth, political connections and the number of ads they sold for the nearly 900-page pageant program." Chu himself called it a "campaign session for some of these girls ... this is totally, 100 percent outside the spectrum of what is supposed to be disclosed. He's not even supposed to be in the room." According to Chu, when he objected to being told to focus on two specific contestants (rather than all of those whose scores placed them in contention), Sanders told him, "Don't mess with it."

Sanders vehemently denied the allegations. Rumors about Chu's behavior during the pageant—including one preposterous story about him hitting on Miss South Carolina's Outstanding Teen in a hot tub—began to work their way around pageant circles. Very few believed those allegations; the Sanders family had burned through most of their political capital by then, and their influence had significantly waned.

Plus, Chu (who, by any empirical assessment, had little to gain by bringing down the Miss South Carolina Pageant) stuck to his story. And more and more media sources picked it up. Four days after the first story was published, MAO announced that Sanders and his wife, Gail, were "retiring."

Perhaps the most striking element of this story, however, wasn't the judge who shouldn't have been there in the first place. Nor was it the possibility that the selection process had been corrupted. The real bombshell was the statement from Sharon Pearce, Miss America's in-house public relations executive (who was, a year later, promoted to vice president, where she would earn a six-figure salary): "'The national organization wants to make sure each state is following the rules and guidelines established' for their respective organizations, she said. 'This is a state issue, and we will certainly look into it. This is a South Carolina issue, and is not related to the Miss America Organization. We'll be happy to look into it.'"

Not related to the Miss America Organization. Sadly, this is not an exception to the rule; it's emblematic of MAO's philosophy regarding its franchisees. It's one of the reasons there's so little turnover among state executive directors, especially those who probably should have gotten their pink slips long ago. Without the organizational skills and/or staff competency to enforce the pageant's own rules, MAO takes every possible opportunity to offload responsibility onto state organizations. This practice means that oversight from MAO itself is severely limited; for example, complaints from volunteers, contestants, and fans—about concerns such as possible corruption or ethical violations—are re-routed to that state's executive director for "investigation" and resolution. Detailed investigation by the national office is usually limited to instances in which the news media pick up the story. But if, for instance, you're a contestant who notices something untoward about your state pageant's proceedings, and if you take the time to sit down and write a letter to the Miss America staff about the situation, chances are that it will land right back in the lap of the state director whose negligence may have led to the very incident you're reporting. It's the equivalent of an external audit being performed on an organization's finances and then reported back to the finance department for dissemination. There will be no consequences, because the buck stops precisely with the person or persons who are the source of the original problem.

Another example: In 2009, current and former volunteers got together to attempt a takeover of one state pageant. Their franchise application included a painstakingly detailed account of alleged abuses by, and grievances against, the executive director of that state's program. The incidents included everything from emotional abuse to failure to pay appropriate taxes on merchandise sold at fund-raisers, and included accounts provided by former state titleholders of their experiences. One titleholder recounted rumors that the director had concocted about her excessive drinking and inappropriate sexual behavior. Another described throwing her arms up in front of her face when she suddenly feared that her boss was going to hit her. Compelling stuff, and about as far as one can get from the stated mission of the Miss America Organization.

MAO staff did nothing. Except to privately characterize it as "character assassination." The board of directors' Franchise Committee reportedly recommended against renewing the state's contract, but were overruled by high-ranking officials.

It takes a great deal of courage to speak up about possible corruption within the Miss America Organization. And most of the time, the consequence of trying to retain the pageant's integrity is that the informer is blacklisted from future participation. For those who have volunteered for years, even decades, with the goal of providing opportunities for the young women who benefit, it's easier to turn a blind eye and continue working on the micro level. No one wants to see the institution collapse. And everyone is afraid to be the one accused of bringing about its failure.

As for George Bauer, he would go the way of his predecessors, Rob Beck and Bob Renneisen, when the pageant was dropped by ABC following the 2004 telecast. Bauer allegedly knew that the network was bailing out shortly after the September show aired, but instead of informing the board, he reportedly went on vacation. In the wake of his departure from the organization, Deidre Downs (2005) would hold the title for an unprecedented fifteen months. Meanwhile, pageant officials scrambled to find a new television partner home for the show.

A fter a wild ride that saw Miss America supervised by—and then waving good-bye to—four CEOs between late 1998 and late 2004, facing massive budgetary challenges and its first bout of network homelessness since the beginning of television, it was the perfect moment for a thorough institutional audit by an outside entity. Had MAO brought in the pros to advise them on reorganizing, eliminating waste and redundancy, and efficiently securing and spending money, it could have had a tremendously positive impact. In fact, it's almost impossible to imagine that an institution in so much trouble on so many fronts could ignore the warning signs—and the problem wasn't simply that the board happened to hire the wrong executives.

But, of course, none of that happened. In fact, a new regime would soon take hold of Miss America's destiny and make it clear that dissenters were less welcome than ever.

THIRTEEN

W hen you've dedicated a great deal of time—a year of your life—and almost always more—to something you love, you don't want to watch it die. In fact, the urge to help, to devote even more hours, to try to right the ship, becomes overwhelming.

A few years after I give up the crown, I find myself in this peculiar position with regard to the Miss America Organization. Fortunately, I have the same belated recognition of kinship that I remember from my isolated year on the road. I realize that there's already an existing network of women who probably care as much as I do, who innately understand the frustration I'm feeling, and who are most likely also trying to figure out how they can help.

For the first time—outside of the usual chitchat and pageant festivities that we share each time we return to Atlantic City, the Miss Americas get together with a different purpose in mind.

Because we're scattered all over the country, we have to communicate virtually, and it doesn't happen overnight. I've started copying and pasting the annual contact information e-mail into a Word document, thinking it will be easier for everyone to find if we need it. Just like that, everyone's *e-mail address is in one "to" box, and we begin to discuss what is happening with—and to—our program.*

I say "our" program not because the Miss Americas own it. We don't. No one owns it, really; it has been created and sustained by a massive effort from hundreds of thousands of people, over the course of nearly a century. But just as those of us who have worn the crown have found ourselves becoming symbols—and, for that matter, targets—the minute the crown perches on our respective heads, we have also been granted a kind of clout that isn't available to everyone who loves Miss America. It is my belief that it's time we get together and put that clout to use.

Miss America has always had outspoken renegades. It is, of course, easier to dismiss one vocal ex–beauty queen than it is to marginalize an entire collective of intelligent, savvy women. Via e-mail, we learn that we have plenty of common concerns. And we make a plan—followed by an appointment—to go to Atlantic City for an audience with the board of directors.

Over the course of weeks, we plan our strategy. A small group of us happens to live in Manhattan, and we take the lead in formulating an approach too compelling for the powers that be to ignore. Susan Powell (1981) has experienced frustration with sponsorship opportunities; she relates the story of meeting some Betty Crocker executives who'd been dying to get involved with Miss America, and trying to explain to them later why the pageant seems to have no interest in bringing them (and their money) on board. "That's just the way they do things" may be true—I'm willing to bet that more phone calls have gone unreturned in that office than at all the other nonprofits in New Jersey put together— but it's still embarrassing. And once a Miss America (or a volunteer or a fan) gets egg on her face a couple times, she stops calling in favors. But sponsorships are something we know we can pull together, if the MAO leadership agrees to handle them properly.

Debbye Turner (1990), Gretchen Carlson (1989), Susan, and I get together more than once at Gretchen's Upper West Side apartment. At this point, Gretchen and Debbye both work at CBS; they know their way around media. Debbye, as the first Miss America in the era of official platform issues, intimately understands the challenges of using substance to gain credibility. Gretchen's husband, Casey, is a successful sports agent, and his company, IMG, has serious power when it comes to branding. And I have a good relationship with one of the most successful publicists in New York, whose wheelhouse is the intersection of politics, philanthropy, and entertainment. And who just happens to be a closet Miss America fan.

With input from the non–New York Miss America contingent, we craft a presentation. We pile into a car and head down the Garden State Parkway. We stride into the offices at the Sheraton—past the bronze statue of Bert Parks that sings "There She Is" when you stand under the crown between his outstretched arms. Around the corner in the lobby. Through the rotunda, where replicas of past Miss Americas' winning gowns beckon from their glass displays and a giant TV screen replays decades of crowning moments in a never-ending loop.

We're pretty sure we're going to kick ass.

Passing through the heavy oak doors, we meet Heather Whitestone (1995) and Evelyn Ay (1954), both of whom have traveled to join us. We wait in the inner lobby, surrounded by oil paintings; each of our official headshots has been painstakingly transferred onto canvas and rests in a wooden frame. If it were your first trip to the Miss America offices, you would look around and think, "Wow. These people really love their Miss Americas."

Unless you're one of those Miss Americas, and you want to help make changes. In that case, things go south pretty quickly.

The meeting gets off to a rocky start. We sit in a line along *one side of the conference table, with the board members occupying the rest. The chairman at the time, a guy named Steve Fuhs, quickly launches into a history lesson about the Miss America Organization. Debbye politely but firmly interrupts, rattling off some key moments in the pageant's evolution: first scholarships awarded, first talent competition. We're not here to be lectured about what Miss America is. We've lived it more completely than anyone else at this table—even the longtime volunteers. We're here to make a real pitch about how the pageant can use its built-in resources to save itself.*

We tell the board members what we can offer them—sponsors, media contacts, turnaround specialists. We will call in our favors. We will mobilize other Miss Americas, most of whom are already fired up. Evelyn gets choked up. Heather cries. It's pretty moving.

And we tell them the only thing we want in return: board representation. It's just stupid that Miss Americas—we who are living, breathing resources with significant experience, energy, and passion—are so underutilized. We don't want to take over. But we also don't want to hang around on the sidelines, waiting to be trotted across the stage once a year. We don't want to simply sign autographs, shake some VIP hands, and then be put back in cold storage for the year. We want to do more than look pretty and sit in the corner while the grown-ups talk. This, and the expectation that the office get its act together and start behaving professionally, is all we ask in return for everything we feel we have to offer.

The meeting ends like this: One of the board members, a small man with a lot of gel in his dark hair, thanks us for our time. He tells us to go ahead and start bringing in the sponsors, and they'll let us know what they decide about the rest of it. And that, as they say, is that.

It is the first time Miss America really breaks my heart. It will not be the last.

It's not a total loss, to be sure—we do succeed in getting board representation. Two seats, to be exact. Later, three. Somewhat predictably, none of us who attended that meeting is among those chosen. If you speak up, you're a threat. If you're not easily managed, it's better for you to be neutralized. You may have ideas and possibilities and excitement burning a hole in your brain, but it's safer for the status quo if you are simply one of many in an evening gown, voicelessly waving from the stage annually as your name and year are announced. After all, the logic goes, you get to come to the pageant every year; it's the one place in the world where you are famous. People know you by your first name. They may whisper, once you turn your back, about how you've aged or the weight you've gained, but they are overjoyed when they first spot you among the crowd. And to many of the decision makers, it seems as if that should be enough to satisfy you. If it's not, too bad. But thanks for playing.

Eventually, one of our little gang actually will be invited onto the board. Gretchen, who has advanced from a CBS substitute anchor to the host of Fox and Friends, gets the call.

In hindsight, I understand the reasoning behind the board's lackluster response to our proposals. At the time, it was a seriously divided body. A single vote could swing the axis of power entirely in one direction or another. I see the writing on the wall pretty soon after the meeting, actually; within a week or two after we make our presentation, the Miss America Organization hires a new PR firm. It's not the publicist I've offered, who represents the breed of Hollywood stars who are so recognizable that they have to hide from their fame. They never even ask for a meeting with him. MAO's new press representatives are based in Egg Harbor City, New Jersey.

After the 2004 pageant, Steve Fuhs and the newest acting CEO, Art McMaster, get busy making some big changes. McMaster is the organization's former comptroller, who has *been on the staff since 1999 and presided over the complete collapse of Miss America's finances. Presumably, he has been promoted to the top job simply because he was the only middle-aged white man in the office left standing; it's hard to imagine that his leadership skills or executive experience is at all compelling. Eventually, he will be made full-time CEO. On more than one occasion, he will ask people to shelve legitimate concerns so that they don't go down in history as the person who killed Miss America. Regardless of the validity of their grievances, this tactic is a winner when deployed effectively. If your love for the pageant outweighs your desire to collect your scholarship money, for example, you are likely to quietly abandon that pursuit.*

An example: Shortly after our meeting, Fuhs and Mc-Master go to a meeting of the Atlantic City Convention and Visitors Authority (ACCVA) and beg out of the pageant's contract. Those who are there report that it's a bit of a guilt trip; MAO has gotten itself into such a dire situation that it can no longer afford to put on the pageant in Atlantic City. Like so many others, the ACCVA doesn't want to be responsible for killing Miss America. But neither does it want to "give them a site fee and pay all the costs and put a million dollars in their pocket," ACCVA executive director Jeffrey Vassar tells the New York Times. *They release the pageant from its obligations, on the condition that "Miss America must continue to appear ten times a year on behalf of the visitors' bureau for the next five years."*

Miss America announces that the pageant will move to Las Vegas, and be televised by Country Music Television in January, rather than in September, as has been traditional. Though the arrangement does decent business for CMT, it lasts for only two years. Sure, Miss America has a heartland appeal that works for much of CMT's audience base, but ultimately the two just aren't compatible enough. CMT says good-bye.

The pageant moves to The Learning Channel, where it

lives for three years. TLC is known for its reality shows, and this is where the whole thing gets really hard to watch. In the first year, TLC creates a multi-episode reality show designed to introduce the contestants to the audience over a longer period than one night. It's an interesting idea, but in practice it doesn't quite work. The contestants arrive for the first episode and are instructed to put on full pageant gear: evening gowns, heels, stage makeup. Then they stand on bleachers for several hours while Stacy and Clinton, the hosts of What Not to Wear, *go through their suitcases and critique their clothes. That year's eventual winner, Kirsten Haglund (2008), doesn't really participate much in the quest for camera time; for the majority of episodes, she simply watches and occasionally comments.*

TLC learns from this. The next year (2009), the state titleholders spend about a month in Los Angeles filming a new and improved reality show. They actually live on the Queen Mary *cruise ship for the duration of the shoot. This one involves challenges that have nothing to do with the actual job of Miss America—running obstacle courses, designing a dress from a piece of black fabric, "working it" on the catwalk. Their participation is encouraged, even practically mandated, by the "golden sashes" awarded to the challenge winners; the women who end up with these sashes will be entered into an audience contest to become the "people's choice" semifinalists at Miss America. Meaning that regardless of how they perform in the preliminary competitions, they may make it to the top fifteen on the basis of how well they glue feathers onto cloth with a timer ticking in the background.*

There are also reportedly plenty of moments in these long, long days (often going from six a.m. until midnight, with not one penny of pay—which frankly doesn't even sound legal) during which the producers try to set up conflict between the women. After the first few days, the contestants revolt and demand a meeting where they can voice their concerns.

They refuse to be part of a show that is constantly trying to pit them against one another ("Miss West Virginia says she's against gay marriage! You're in favor of gay marriage; what do you think of her?!?") The producers relent; the Miss America executives profess ignorance and horror that these things are going on at all.

The end result is that when the contestants go home after this experience, more than a handful of them wonder how they can possibly look little girls in the eye and encourage them to compete for Miss America when they grow up. For women who have spent years, in some cases, trying to get to this point, that's a remarkable change in perspective.

Here's the thing: I'm not opposed to reality shows in the slightest. They can be fun. I watch them. But what bothers me is that these women did not sign up for this. If you're on The Bachelor, *or* Wipeout, *or* Survivor, *it's because you went through a long and usually arduous application process to get there. These women signed up to compete for the title of Miss America. They didn't sign up for a reality show.*

And the other problem with the reality-show approach, aside from the fact that it cheapens the whole event, is that these women are not good television. Not in the Real Housewives *way, anyway. Even the least-experienced ones have been somewhat groomed to appear diplomatic, thoughtful, intelligent, passionate about community service. If I had a dollar for every Miss State who was likely to go on national television and thoughtlessly talk trash about another contestant (much less flip over a table or start a food fight), I would never, ever have any dollars. There's a code of etiquette that's been present at Miss America ever since Lenora Slaughter gathered the wives of Atlantic City's most prominent gentlemen and turned them into the Hostess Committee. There may be bitchiness, sure, but it's covered and disguised and passive-aggressive. Very few will walk up to someone and say, "You look like a slut in that dress." They're more likely to say, "Wow, that dress is a really brave choice!" with a big smile. And this is when the cameras aren't rolling. Put them on television, and they're even less likely to misbehave. They're just too savvy and image-conscious by the time they get to this level.*

Miss America is not a reality show. And any attempts to make it one just feel wrong. Because when you get into reality-show territory, someone has to be the butt of the joke. It's totally disingenuous to talk about celebrating young women, giving them scholarships and encouraging them to be leaders, while at the same time you're looking for the ones whom America can laugh at. Even the more minor reality-show tweaks can be totally disheartening to the women, and it's not because they refuse to play ball. They will ordinarily twist themselves into bedazzled pretzels to give the pageant what it's asking for. So when even the contestants are checking out left and right, it's hard to imagine how uncomfortable the TV viewers must feel.

In all honesty, the reality-show stuff doesn't start in the Vegas era. Nor does relegating the "fabulous, beautiful, intelligent" contestants to the bottom of the priority list. The pageant has sold out these women repeatedly over the years in the name of television. It's just that the Vegas years lay it bare.

What's really happened is this: at a certain point, the Miss America Organization has decided that it's an awful lot of work to sell the commercial time for the pageant telecast. It's easier for the network to do it. On some level this makes sense.

But it comes with a built-in problem. If you hand over the recruitment and securing of sponsors to the TV people, you no longer have the sponsors to act as a buffer between your organization and some producer who wants two talents on TV (2004). Or video clips before the swimsuit competition of the contestants, Star Search *spokesmodel-style, lounging around candlelit hot tubs in bikinis, suggestively running a hand up their thigh (also 2004). Or a* Jeopardy-*style quiz*

185

for the top five finalists, with questions that most eighth-graders could answer (2000, 2001, 2002). Or a "casual wear" competition, which communicates the message that external appearance is even more important than it has been in the past.

If you have sponsors in your corner, you can say this to the network: "Wow, we would love to have those hot tub video clips! Such an amazing idea! Unfortunately, our corporate partners say that that's not what they signed on for. What else would you like to try?" You can retain control of your own brand while someone else is the bad guy. If you don't have the third-party bad guy, and you don't have the money to produce the show yourself, you effectively hand over control of the whole shebang to the network executives. And they don't have the history, or the understanding, that you do. And they don't really care about building your brand, or reinforcing your interesting and complicated identity. They just want eyeballs on the screen.

Problematic, huh?

TLC dumps the pageant after the crowning of Miss America 2010. The show has put up good ratings, particularly in key demographics. But MAO wants a three-year contract, so they say, and TLC wants to pay less to televise the show.

As usual, the pageant is caught out by the news. There's never been a television breakup—not a single, solitary one—that the MAO has been out in front of. The headline always includes some word like "dump" or "drop." Judging simply by the punctuation and spelling errors in MAO's typical press releases, it seems that functional competence in PR savvy and spin is way beyond the abilities of the marketing director. Who, by the way, makes about $125,000 in 2011.

The crazy thing is that so many people stay involved, despite all this chaos. Everyone thinks the magic bullet is right around the corner. They have seen what Miss America can do for a contestant. When you volunteer your time, you can literally watch a girl turn into a woman. She figures out who she is, how to express herself, what she thinks of what's going on in the world, how to occupy space onstage, what impact she plans to have on her community. She grows out of being her parents' daughter and evolves into her own autonomous human being. And you get to be a part of that. It's a tremendous honor, and the experience is worth every second of time you can possibly volunteer.

And then you watch her go to Miss America, the biggest moment of her life. And if she doesn't make the top fifteen, she is sent to sit with the other non-finalists in what the fans call the "Losers' Lounge," and stagehands offer her donuts on a silver platter. Literally, donuts. On, literally, a silver platter. That single visual catapults the pageant backwards. Because MAO contradicts its own message that it's "Lifestyle and Fitness" competition, not the "Swimsuit" competition, by implying (and sometimes outright saying) that the contestants have all been starving themselves.

Each year, the contestants have to fill out a questionnaire *for use by the production company. Favorite movie, your secret wish, what you like to do in your spare time. And each year, producers cherry-pick these factoids for various uses. Some girls don't put much time into it, choosing to bang out some quick answers so they can get through their paperwork—there's a lot of paperwork—and move on to other areas of their preparation. I'm more inclined to believe that when you're applying for a six-figure job, you'd better make sure that every bit of background you provide about yourself is informative, interesting, and helps to effectively brand you for the people (a.k.a. the judges) who decide whether or not you get that job. Most of the time, for instance, they ask "what is the one thing you can't live without?" If I had ten bucks for every first draft that contains a response like "OMG, my BlackBerry!" I could probably buy enough Black-Berry stock to run the company. When I help contestants develop their paperwork, that question is my favorite target. Anyone who literally can't live without their cell phone is not someone I want to hire, unless perhaps I'm hiring people to work at Verizon. I place a lot of emphasis on these little throwaways, because you never know when and where the information is going to surface.*

But even if you spend hours putting together a smart, strategic questionnaire, you just can't control everything. You have to anticipate how the information could be used to embarrass you, either accidentally or intentionally. My friend Leigh-Taylor Smith is third runner-up to Miss America 2009. She's from a relatively well-off family, so we make sure to highlight the (many) things about her that indicate that she's real, grounded, compassionate, and curious about people from all walks of life. Like the fact that she's visited a correctional facility and spent time talking with a group of inmates about what might have helped them make different choices. During this visit, she, her chaperone, and some of the inmates are actually in tears as they recount the loss of years of their lives. And then, there it is, as soon as she starts singing a romantic ballad on national television: a pop-up on the screen reading "She has performed in a prison!" Chelsea Handler, on her popular late-night E! show, has a field day with this little gem.

The problem isn't just poor judgment about how the contestants are portrayed. Sure, that factoid is comically incompatible with the visual metaphor of Leigh-Taylor's talent performance, which has been crafted very carefully. Ultimately, though, it's just another example of valuable information presented poorly.

But many times the cognitive dissonance can be stultifying. To put it mildly, MAO simply doesn't do well with managing its message. The leadership is continually frustrated by the fact that Those Cynical Media People focus on pageant stereotypes, rather than the real opportunities Miss America provides for young women. And yet the organiza-

tion fails, time and time again, to synthesize these objectives with the information it's putting out into the world.

Leigh-Taylor's successor, Alyse, once asks my advice about a question she's been wrestling with; the year she competes (2010), they ask every contestant to submit a favorite recipe. My response: "While you're at it, make sure to tell them about your ideal first date, and the secret to getting really, really streak-free windows!" The media will always latch on to stuff like this, because it's more buzzy—and easier to mock—than statistics about scholarship dollars and how many miles per month Miss America travels. They "tell" those things, but they simultaneously "show" stereotypes being reinforced left and right.

I don't know how many times I've seen pageant-related specials on any number of channels, but I do know this: if you set an egg timer, the people on your TV screen will be talking about those stultifying pageant beauty secrets before it goes off. Butt glue, duct tape, Preparation H. It's one thing when it's a third party; it's nearly impossible to control how that plays out. But the 2013 telecast is immediately preceded by a one-hour 20/20 special about what goes on behind the scenes when you're competing for Miss America. In my opinion, these forty-odd minutes of TV time single-handedly set the pageant back twenty years. There is teasing of hair; there's almost-but-not-quite-bitchy conversation among the contestants. And, nestled on its typically hallowed and much-discussed perch, there is butt glue. For some reason, people never fail to be fascinated that these women spray on sports adhesive so that their swimsuits will stay put, instead of riding up in the back while they walk across the stage. The 20/20 special, titled "Pageant: Confidential," ups the ante; presumably because the mere discussion of this phenomenon is way too dignified, they actually show a backstage volunteer attending to one young lady after another, assembly-line style. Having watched MAO struggle to reinvent the pageant's image over and over again, I cringe. It's so embar-

rassing, and so damaging, and so, so typical. And the truly unfortunate part of all this? Because the show's been done with the pageant's cooperation, MAO has actually had a say in what's made the final cut. The Huffington Post headline, for example, doesn't say "Miss America Is Really All About the Scholarships" or "Wow, Miss America Ain't Kidding About All That Community Service!" Nope, it reads "Miss America Beauty Secrets: Butt Glue and Lots of Tape." It goes on to show Miss West Virginia discussing how to actually lift one's posterior by tucking it properly into one's swimsuit, noting that applying the glue itself is "an art." Brilliant.

Messaging has always been a problem, and will continue to be one until there's a major change of personnel. Another example: in 2008, I have a bit of a falling-out with the national office. I'm doing the Broadway show Legally Blonde, and MAO's marketing director, Sharon Pearce, asks me to be one of the three Miss Americas to appear on a karaoke show called Don't Forget the Lyrics. Sounds fun, and whatever we win will go to the scholarship fund. I agree to use my days off to fly to L.A. for the filming. But just in case something goes wrong and the schedule changes, I ask if I can wear a Legally Blonde shirt on the show. So that if my return trip gets delayed (not unheard of in the TV world) and they have to put my understudy on for the matinee, at least our producers will feel like they've gotten something out of it.

It is then that I find out that we're expected to wear evening gowns.

Evening gowns. On a karaoke game show.

I try to compromise. Cocktail dress? Nope. The producers say they want the visual of three beautiful "queens" (which apparently MAO is no longer trying to correct), and—I will never forget these words—"Kirsten [the current Miss America], of course, will be wearing her crown." Oh, okay, so it's gowns and a crown. On a karaoke game show. Spectacular.

I keep trying to negotiate this. I tell them that if it's a deal *breaker for the game-show people, I'm happy to step aside and let someone else do it. There are Miss Americas who would wear a chicken suit in exchange for some face time on national television.*

Eventually, I find myself sitting in Sharon Pearce's office with her, and with Art McMaster. And it really does look like the gown thing is mandatory, which means I'm just not going to do this. As politely as I can, I tell them that I'm not going to do them a two-day favor and fly across the country to, in essence, reinforce the number-one stereotype people have about Miss America: that regardless of the appropriateness for any particular occasion, she shows up in a gown and crown. I know this, of course, because I've done Q&As in countless high school assemblies, and more often than not, a kid raises his or her hand and expresses surprise that I haven't walked in wearing a gown. In the school gym. So, no, I'm not going to show up on a game show in one. Dressy, fine. Sparkly, fine. No gown. And I tell them that frankly, I'm kind of surprised to be the first one who's thought of this. I do not tell them what I really think, which is that they're so desperate for exposure that they'll ask their Miss Americas and their contestants to do anything, and expect to be thanked for the opportunity. And that they have no message. And that this is why they can't build a brand that sponsors and TV networks will get behind.

I do not say these things. Art and Sharon still look at me like I have two heads. They seriously don't understand why I have an objection to this.

A note: In 2011, these two people make about $400,000 in combined salary. The pageant as a whole reports total revenue of −$165,927. Failing upward, indeed.

In fact, Miss America's 2011 tax returns indicate that Art McMaster makes $252,136 per year. Of course, the same return indicates that more than $720,000 (with no corresponding revenue listed) has been expended to "provide support and related expenses for Miss America to promote *awareness of her annual charitable cause." It's a remarkable sum, given that the winner herself (who is classified as an independent contractor, despite a job description specifying that she is expected to be "on-call twenty-four hours a day, seven days a week, for the duration of her time as Miss America") makes about $10,000 per month, receives no benefits, and has her travel expenses and those of her tour manager paid by the sponsors that invite her to their events. It doesn't do much good to question these numbers, though; true to his background as comptroller, McMaster himself signs off on the tax returns.*

O ver these same years I watch as MAO forces NAMASP to disband. My friends who know about this stuff (I do a stint as a vice president of our union, Actors' Equity) say that this is a questionable legal move. It could be argued that NAMASP is a union, and that dismantling it—by forbidding franchisees to belong to an outside organization—would not be looked upon kindly by the Department of Labor. You can't union-bust just because the members in question happen to be volunteers.

I watch them chase people out of the organization after they stand up and object to the way things are being done. I watch them blackball my friends. I watch contestants get caught in the crossfire between warring factions. I watch them make up the rules as they go along.

I sit in the audience and watch people roll their eyes as staff members and board members are featured onstage at pageant preliminaries in Vegas. Nothing wrong with the honchos saying a few words, of course. Except that on almost every occasion, those "few words" last, oh, thirty to forty-five minutes. People actually look forward to these speeches, so that they can hit the restroom. Or the bar. Or, hey, both! I've heard the emcee read executive bios that last twice as long as it takes for a girl to perform her talent. One year, it ac-

tually becomes a bit. The host stops talking after a while to ask for a bottle of water. Talks some more. Requests a chair. Sits down, keeps reading. A stagehand comes out and dabs her forehead with a handkerchief. The audience roars with laughter.

The next year, said host is conspicuously absent from the pageant.

I end up doing what most people do after they're disappointed enough times. I find that I have a lot less enthusiasm for fighting the good fight. And anyway, most of the people on the other side play dirty pool. So before I even pick up the cue stick, I know I'll lose. I just spend less time around Miss America. If you don't put your heart, your goodwill, your purity of spirit out there, it's much easier to keep from getting hurt. And I like to give people the benefit of the doubt and all, but enough's enough. You know, it's the old "fool me once" adage. Except I let them fool me, all in all, dozens and dozens of times. Shame on me, right?

What it comes down to, really, is that there are two types of people involved with Miss America. There are those who are in it for the advancement of young women. Even if their version of that doesn't involve teaching someone to articulate the nuances of America's public school problems, or the situation in the Middle East, or how we can keep kids off drugs. Even if they just like to watch the way a girl's posture and carriage and self-worth improve when she puts on a really beautiful gown. They like being around that progress, which is truly a lovely thing to witness. They want to make the world better, and their community better, one young woman at a time. I know that sounds like a really Miss America thing to say, but I wouldn't say it if I hadn't seen it over and over again.

And the other type of person lets someone else do all that work, then uses Miss America as both literal and metaphorical arm candy.

The arm candy group has mastered the parlance that

means the most to the ones who love helping young women. In fact, they count on that goodwill to keep people in line. Sometimes, it seems like Miss America—the institution, not the individual—has been taken hostage. They strategically place her in the middle of conflict; they position her as "under assault" when the status quo is threatened. They get away with it specifically because of the very love these volunteers have for the pageant. And thus the status quo doesn't improve. In fact, as the arm candy people have more success with their manipulative tactics, the status quo actually gets worse and worse and worse.

Dysfunction, like corruption, like addiction, flourishes in secrecy. Sooner or later, somebody has to decide that it's time—as Keanu Reeves says in the movie Speed—*to shoot the hostage. Because if you take away the hostage-taker's leverage, if you disable his ability to drag everyone else down with his selfish agenda, you have a snowball's chance of resolving the situation with relatively little collateral damage. In the case of Miss America, when reason, negotiation, and attempts to collaborate are routinely met with platitudes, stonewalling, and outsized personal attacks, there comes a point when someone just has to blow the roof off the joint and hope that exposing the misdeeds will provide a path toward correcting them. It's not a perfect scenario—in fact, it's pretty far down the list of ideal options—but sometimes, it's the only way to save what you love.*

FOURTEEN

To the casual observer, the past couple of years seem to have been more successful ones for America's oldest pageant.

In 2010, after the embarrassing split with TLC, MAO announced that it had reached a deal with ABC to broadcast the 2011 pageant. It was a surprise, to say the least, to those who felt that network television would never again darken Miss America's doorstep. Despite relatively strong ratings performances in the preceding few years on CMT and TLC, the celebration among pageant fans was marked by one specific question: how had they managed to pull this off?

A day or two later, the answer presented itself. The first red flag appeared in the *Variety* story announcing the three-year deal, when Sam Haskell—whose election as board chairman had initially indicated significant promise, as he was the former Worldwide Head of Television for the William Morris Agency—"declined to comment on ABC's new license fee."

As it turned out, Haskell had good reason to be coy: it was a time buy. Unlike in years past, ABC would not be paying for the rights to televise the pageant. The network would *be* paid by advertisers and sponsors for the privilege of using its airwaves to televise *Miss America*. As a point of reference, ABC paid a reported $5.6 million for its last telecast in 2004. Under the new arrangement, MAO— and whatever sponsors it could recruit—would have to foot the bill.

Although there was some "gotcha"-type crowing when the media discovered the nature of the deal, the return to ABC was widely regarded as a net positive. And some sponsorships did, in fact, come to fruition. Over the next couple of years, several large companies would come to the party. DSW, Amway, Express, and others saw opportunities for product tie-ins. Most of these relationships didn't last more than a year or so, although Amway continued to provide funding (and contestants continued to shoot promotional videos about their favorite "Artistry by Amway" lip gloss) until 2013. The sponsorship dance has been relatively unfocused and random: since 2009, Miss America has hawked environmentally friendly water bottles, the dairy industry, vitamins, shoes, children's bedroom furniture shaped like stiletto heels, and—wait for it—a custom seasoning, with her face on the bottle, sold primarily at the Indiana State Fair. For those of us who lean toward the thoughtful end of the spectrum, that one was particularly hard to swallow. Pun intentional. In most cases, it doesn't feel like strategic alignment based on synthesized brand identity. It feels more like they'll send Miss America out to talk about any company that will throw a few bucks into the kitty.

But at least sponsors have materialized. Although some of them haven't stuck around for very long, the flow of resources is critically necessary. Around the time of the move to Vegas, the pageant was so far in the red that the leadership had very few options. As a response, a partnership was developed with Children's Miracle Network Hospitals. Under the terms of the agreement, Miss America herself would serve as a Goodwill Ambassador for CMN during her year. This was not a new designation; past Miss Americas have held the same title.

Here's what *did* break some ground: for the first time ever, the contestants would have to "pay to play," by raising a specific sum in order to advance through the competition. In order to enter a local pageant, the required donation to CMN is $100; for a state, $250. Unlike Donald Trump's rival for-profit Miss USA Pageant, where entry fees range from a few hundred dollars to thousands, Miss America has always prided itself on not charging an entry fee. With the advent of the CMN project, MAO manages to avoid the entry-fee label, while still reaping a significant payoff. Additionally, special awards (called "Miracle Maker" awards) have been created for the contestants who raise the most money. Some do go well above and beyond; a recent Miss Ohio, for example, put together a bike tour. She crisscrossed her state on two wheels and raised thousands of dollars.

There is, as it happens, a benefit for Miss America as well.

Of the money raised by the contestants, MAO gets a significant split, reportedly as much as 60 percent. The original plan dictated a layered payout to the local and state pageants. But for a while, these organizations could claim that money only if they were a recognized 501(c)(3) program, and in the last few years it has become increasingly difficult for any group with the word "pageant" in its name to obtain this designation. As a result, the national office has retained most of MAO's split of the CMN dollars.

Is it a little shady to have thousands of contestants soliciting money for seriously ill children, when a large percentage finances the pageant they're competing in? Probably. But as a high-ranking official privately said when the partnership was developed, it happened because there was simply no other choice. If not for the CMN dollars, the pageant would have gone under. And really, if nothing's sacred, what's the problem with covering the operating costs under the banner of kids with cancer?

As for the platform issue, it has largely become a thing of the past . . . at least at the national level. Each contestant is still required to create a platform issue in order to compete for Miss America titles. And the outcome of the national competition is at least partly dependent upon which young woman makes the most persuasive case for how she plans to make an impact with her activism.

But during her actual year with the crown, Miss America's individual platform issue is largely abandoned. The new talking points have everything to do with scholarship and little to do with causes, and the new breed of appearances focuses far more heavily on promoting the sponsors.

The irony, of course, is that the platform issue is an obvious solution to what ails Miss America. It's a valuable resource if promoted correctly. Even Donald Trump has come to recognize that public service equals inherent value. Although they aren't asked to develop individual platforms per se, his titleholders (Miss Universe, Miss USA, and Miss Teen USA) now have their own activist agendas. Every Miss Universe focuses on HIV/AIDS issues, Miss USA targets breast and ovarian cancer charities, and Miss Teen USA works to promote anti-bullying and self-esteem initiatives. In August 2010, Miss Universe, Ximena Navarrete, was discussing her work with AIDS charities on NBC's *Today*. Navarrete, like many other Miss Universe titleholders, traveled extensively to promote AID for AIDS, Gay Men's Health Crisis, and a number of other HIV/AIDS-specific organizations.

Meanwhile, Caressa Cameron (Miss America 2010) had a lifelong commitment to AIDS service and prevention.

Cameron's uncle had died of AIDS, and she had witnessed the struggles of an HIV-positive child fostered by her family. Her judging panel, which included conservative radio host Rush Limbaugh, enthusiastically endorsed her as a valuable asset to her generation; Limbaugh, who surprised many pageant fans by becoming an outspoken supporter of a liberal African American AIDS activist, said afterward, "She has it all. Extraordinarily good conversationalist, amazing presence, unique and classic beauty, glamour ... and the girl can sing!!" Cameron—who became an AIDS volunteer at age nine—went on to work for AIDS United, a national organization based in Washington, DC.

A review of her year, however, reveals that very little of her time was spent on her passion project. The official MAO press releases proclaim headlines like "Miss America 2010 Celebrates National Pancake Day!" "Miss America Cools Off the Summer Heat on [Dairy Queen's] Miracle Treat Day!" and "Tune In Alert: Miss America 2010 on Pageant Talk Radio TOMORROW." *Not one* of MAO's fifty-odd press releases during Cameron's year has a headline mentioning HIV/AIDS. While Miss Universe was promoting AIDS education in the Dominican Republic and Panama during her year, Miss America was in Columbus, Ohio; "Miss America Youth Collection Debuts" detailed the October 25 launch of the girls' bedroom furniture line at Value City ... an event that also featured Miss America 1971, Phyllis George.

Certainly, the press releases don't tell the whole story. A deeper search on Cameron indicates that she did, in fact, participate in some platform-related activities. The point here, however, is that though those events may have taken place, and though Cameron undoubtedly used her Limbaugh-endorsed speaking skills to leave an impression on her audience, the MAO office did not promote them as major occasions. IHOP's National Pancake Day is a nationwide event that raises millions of dollars for the Children's Miracle Network. But if the pageant is trying to shore up its brand, shouldn't headlining a World AIDS Day conference at Howard University be as valuable as showing up in a crown to flip some pancakes?

In fact, none of the eight Miss Americas crowned in Las Vegas did much visible work with their platform issues. In many ways, it was as if the pageant simply decided that the execution of a platform-specific year required too much work. Here and there, they got opportunities, and occasionally attracted some favorable press (especially right after their respective crownings). But in most cases, the media seemed to gravitate toward those platforms that developed from individual personal narratives—Kirsten Haglund's recovery from anorexia, Laura Kaeppaeler's father's imprisonment for a white-collar crime—rather than to be mobilized by an organized, top-down campaign focusing on each winner's commitment to public service.

Although she no longer spends 90 percent of her time engaged in activism, Miss America still travels quite a lot. The old reliable "20,000 miles a month" statistic, calculated by Debbye Turner (1990), is trotted out regularly in interviews. And the salary structure, implemented around the time of the move from Atlantic City, incentivizes the office even more intensely to keep her moving. Gone are the days when Miss America collected the bulk of her appearance fees (less a 15 to 20 percent agent-type commission). At thousands of dollars per appearance, she can literally pay off her $10,000-a-month salary in just a couple of days; the salary approach ultimately translates to far more income for the pageant. It should again be noted, however, that the pageant built a significant reserve under the platform-era pay structure. Even with more gross income from Miss America's appearances, MAO has been barely covering its operating expenses for years.

In February 2013, a bombshell: Miss America was leaving Las Vegas and returning to her roots in Atlantic City. Convention Hall—now known as Boardwalk Hall—would once again host the pageant, and it would move back to mid-September, instead of the January crowning date familiar to pageant-in-Vegas fans. Mallory Hagan, the first Miss America from New York since Vanessa Williams, would serve for only eight months; as a result of savvy contract negotiations on her part (and the foresight to have her post-crowning contract reviewed by a corporate attorney), she would be paid her monthly salary for a full year.

Pageant fans, for the most part, were stoked. There was a sense of rightness about the relocation. The online message board communities responded by posting dozens of vintage photos: the long runway, the cavernous hall packed to the rafters, one weepy, moving crowning after another.

Even Art McMaster—who probably didn't mean to throw shade on Las Vegas, but managed to do it anyway—was glowing: "It was always my dream that this would return here," he said. "Sadly, this organization went west for a while. That sadness is over. We are back to the city where the Miss America pageant began, where the Miss America pageant was raised, and where the Miss America pageant belongs." Tactless, yet heartfelt—which, frankly, could serve as an MAO mantra.

In the days to follow, it would become apparent that the move was something of a perfect circle. Hurricane Sandy had devastated the Jersey Shore in October 2012. This was a coordinated effort by government, the public, and yes, Atlantic City businesspeople to declare that the seaside resort was open for business beyond Labor Day. It would also come to light that the break in the case, as it were, was orchestrated by a longtime volunteer; Lieutenant Governor Kim Guadagno, acting on behalf of Governor Chris Christie, had called up the pageant's head of security to arrange a meeting with the MAO brass. Don Wadsworth, a former FBI agent whom Guadagno recalled from her days as a prosecutor, made it happen.

For those in the know, though, the deal carried a bittersweet tinge. Rumors had been circulating for months that both CEO Art McMaster and Vice President Sharon Pearce would be departing the pageant offices, and that Miss America's central headquarters would be relocating to New York. The news of the Atlantic City return certainly had the potential to make this less likely. A Las Vegas pageant had no good reason to retain office space in Linwood, New Jersey; an Atlantic City pageant did. The possible overhaul of the staff—in the name of efficiency, transparency, and good faith—was less likely.

Two months later, the news broke that MAO would be getting $7.3 million in subsidies for bringing the annual event back to the shore. The funding, spread over the three years of the pageant's new contract, is roughly triple the amount Miss America received in 2004, her last year on the Boardwalk. True to the promise from Governor Christie and Lieutenant Governor Guadagno, this money did not include taxpayer dollars; it was reported to be a joint effort between the Atlantic City Convention and Visitors Authority (ACCVA) and the Casino Reinvestment Development Authority (CRDA). And it came at a pivotal moment for Atlantic City's economy. Despite significant citywide redevelopment efforts over the preceding decade, the casino industry had been struggling. Trump Plaza had just been sold for a reported $20 million, the lowest price ever for a casino property (shortly thereafter, the mortgage holder blocked the deal, asserting that the price was too low). And the high-end Revel resort—opened just a year earlier—was already involved in bankruptcy proceedings. Clearly, Atlantic City was looking for something to spur tourism and spending, and estimated that the return of the pageant and its satellite events would attract "129,200 people to the resort. Those people are expected to spend more than $32 million in Atlantic City." The CRDA authorized a $5 million investment, with the ACCVA topping it off with another $2.3 million, spread over a three-year contract.

Additionally, there was a ray of sunshine regarding the platform issue. Miss America 2013, Mallory Hagan, was the second consecutive winner to gain increased traction with her personal crusade. In late April, MAO issued a press release announcing a joint appearance between Hagan and Miss America 1958, Marilyn Van Derbur, both of whom work to stop child sexual abuse.

And finally, there were staff changes—both positive and questionable. Rumors abounded that Chairman of the Board Sam Haskell was no longer willing to do his work for MAO without compensation, although it would be surprising if he—as a onetime highly successful and effective L.A. talent agent—hadn't been collecting fees for brokering sponsorship deals, or as a credited executive producer of the telecast. At the very least, he had utilized MAO's national network to promote his memoir, *Promises I Made My Mother*, and provided incentives to those state franchises that hosted signings or sold copies of the book during their competition weeks.

Ultimately, Haskell took Art McMaster's job. McMaster "retired" soon after the announcement of the pageant's return to Atlantic City. In the wake of his departure, Sharon Pearce was promoted yet again. Despite a less-than-stellar record at essentially every aspect of her previous job (media relations, outreach, proofreading), Pearce would become the new president of the Miss America Organization.

For his part, Sam Haskell succeeded where Leonard Horn had not: he managed to position himself as both chairman of the board (employer) and CEO (employee), a move that Sandra Miniutti of the independent watchdog group Charity Navigator strongly criticized. "The whole point of a board of directors and with a chair is that the person who runs the organization has to be accountable to somebody. You can't be accountable to yourself." According to Miss America's 2012 tax returns, the MAO board had also agreed to pay Haskell's consulting firm $500,000 for his past services—in a year when the organization was $430,000 in the red. *The Press of Atlantic City*'s Jennifer Bogdan interviewed Haskell and Pearce, noting that no chairman of Miss America's board had ever been compensated for that volunteer position.

Haskell shrugged it off, both in Bogdan's article and in a subsequent letter to the state organizations. Both he and Pearce "blamed the deficit on the fact that the organization had not properly accounted for putting on two competitions in one year"—even though the two competitions in question actually occurred in 2013, not the 2012 tax year. As for the $500,000 ($400,000 of which was deferred indefinitely), Haskell asserted that the rest of the board members "felt I had been taken advantage of for seven years. I've got all the network negotiations and all the advertising negotiations . . . I have really good friends on the board who decided it's time for me to get something, you know?" And he explained his CEO contract simply by saying that his salary was not a set number, but only what MAO could afford to pay him. Charity Navigator's Miniutti, in what can only be described as an understatement, called the arrangement "problematic." Unmentioned in the article are the rampant rumors that there was no board vote on whether Haskell would take the job of CEO while remaining chairman of the board—the very individual with the most power to decide what any organization "can afford" to pay its executive. It was indeed a maneuver worthy of his Hollywood roots.

Where the Miss America Organization goes from here is anybody's guess. A strong case could be made that the pageant will continue down the same path that it has been traveling for many years, one that is reactive and marked by mismanagement on both the staff and the board levels. Another argument is that the move back to Atlantic City, the infusion of funding, and the network television presence will spark a top-down reinvention of the brand. There is certainly plenty of goodwill at the moment with regard to Miss America, and her heartland appeal has never completely gone away.

The most likely scenario is probably somewhere in the middle. The board of directors has so far not demonstrated an overwhelming urge to fix what ails the pageant. And as long as its members hear of the daily goings-on through the filter of those with vested interests (i.e., the salaried staff) the board will be unable to get a comprehensive read on where the dysfunction—and, more to the point, the potential—of the Miss America Organization lies.

Throughout the pageant's nearly century-long history, there have certainly been hard times. There have been autocratic leaders, transformational Miss Americas, and above all, the volunteers, contestants, and fans who believe in the possibility that this institution can help to make the world better. But that belief doesn't mean it just happens.

History is littered with the remains of well-intentioned entities that, for one reason or another, just couldn't get their act together. If Miss America is to avoid a permanent place among them—and the hope, certainly, is that she will—she'll have to save herself.

Perhaps the greatest irony of Miss America's complicated history is the lesson she now must learn, one that the second-wave feminist movement sought to teach all women: No matter who you are, you have choices. And you'd best take a good hard look in the mirror and identify the choices that will benefit you in the long run. Because no matter what you've learned to believe, there's nobody riding in on a white horse to save you.

EPILOGUE

Trying to summarize the cultural legacy of the Miss America Organization—especially as it relates to the sweeping changes in women's lives since 1921— is a challenging task. An attempt to predict what Miss America will look like over the coming decades, however, is even more difficult. The internal struggles of the institution, and its unpredictable, often illogical leadership decisions, do not indicate a sunshine-and-unicorns future.

Many, many "pageant people" like to blame MAO's travails on external forces beyond its control. They point to the sheer number of available TV channels as the factor that degrades the ratings, while conveniently ignoring that plenty of quality shows attract viewers simply by being smart and well-crafted productions. Reality shows, scripted comedies and dramas, special events, documentaries—truly, it can be said that in 2014, American viewers can actually be counted on to actively seek out what they want to watch, as well as decide when they want to watch it.

Pageant people believe that the Big Bad Women's Movement is to blame for the decline of Miss America. While it's true that the kind of mom-and-pop innocence on which

Miss America capitalized for decades has become largely (and sadly) obsolete, the organization has had many years to create a powerful message framed by third-wave feminism and the rights of young women to advance their fortunes through all available marketable skills, including their sex appeal. But Miss America has always been reluctant to leverage that particular capital, even as the telecast's visuals and commentary make a convincing case that sex sells. In truth, the messy third-wave debate as a whole—tied as it is to very un-Miss America commodities, like pornography—is a tough nut to crack, let alone control. The platform issue had Miss America knocking on the door of cultural relevance with more force than at any time since Betty Friedan wrote *The Feminine Mystique*, generating positive press coverage and a substantive body of work. Sure, it would always be tough going to make believers out of skeptics. But the journey down the toughest road can lead to the greatest rewards.

These days, the pageant simply doesn't do much to brand itself except put young women in crowns on television. The abundance of competitors and reality shows that portray pageants as catty, demeaning, altogether unpleasant enterprises make it more important than ever for the pageant to project a strong message. Young women who see *Toddlers and Tiaras* or the *Miss Universe* skin show don't understand what makes Miss America different . . . and for its part, the Miss America Organization does a pretty poor job of separating itself from the pack. In fact, MAO has become such a revolving door of sponsors and *their* pet projects that it's hard to discern any mission or message at all. Miss America is here, there, and everywhere. She's at Dairy Queen hustling Blizzards, she's at Value City hawking furniture, she's pushing a cosmetic line and a clothing line and STEM education for girls. She's at a supermarket, gathering change that supposedly benefits sick kids, but a hefty portion of which actually pays the six-figure salaries of the company execs. She's basically selling the familiarity of the Miss America name and celebrating her own Miss America-ness . . . but to anyone with a few minutes to think about it, there's just not much "there" there. Meanwhile, the little girls who used to aspire to wear the crown are dreaming of becoming CEOs instead. Or PhDs. Or sitting behind their very own desk in the Oval Office.

The craziest part is that many, many, many great ideas have come along over the years. Frank Deford offered a gem in 1971, when he suggested dispensing with the nightly preliminary swimsuit and talent awards and just advancing the highest scorers directly to the Saturday-night finals. Even today, a change like that could amp up media attention throughout pageant week, and most of the preliminary winners make the cut anyway. His persuasive case for the move, however, went the way of most well-reasoned, strategic ideas—which is to say, nowhere at all. If the good ideas take the form of potential sponsorships, those sponsors eventually just get frustrated and stop offering their support. A common complaint is MAO's habit of not responding to phone calls, faxes, and requests in a timely, professional manner, whether those overtures are coming from big corporations or local organizations seeking to bring Miss America to their events. In 2010, Caressa Cameron's mother pulled enough strings to get her daughter invited to the White House; when she passed the opportunity along to the office staff, they exchanged e mails among themselves making fun of her. And accidentally cc'd her on their mockery.

The biggest problem Miss America faces is not that the public is distracted by other TV shows, or even that they've moved on to seek other paradigms and goals for their daughters. It's that the public is smart enough to see that MAO is not selling what it says it is. Every year the telecast offers platitudes attesting that the contestants are beautiful, talented, accomplished, and worthy of America's undying respect. And within minutes, sometimes even seconds, the hosts are gabbing outside the dressing room about how many girls are naked as they frantically change for the next competition. The telecast (for most of the country the dominant image of the organization each year) takes an experience that creates genuine camaraderie among the young women—truly, going through the Miss America crucible together bonds many of these women for life—and portrays it as a dog-eat-dog competition. Producers and hosts say that the swimsuit competition is about fitness and health, but they always, always, always ask the contestants how hungry they are. And then give them donuts onstage. And undermine the entire message they've just defined.

Technology has changed Miss America in many ways. Perhaps the pageant's most relevant technological obstacle these days is the abundance of online communities where the hive mind (along with plenty of armchair cultural commentators) can dissect this sloppy game of "show" versus "tell." And once the collective consciousness gets a whiff of hypocrisy, degradation, or condescension, it sure does get harder to reclaim credibility. Assuming, of course, that MAO even wants to do so. Evidence to the contrary suggests otherwise.

Friends on the inside have told me confidentially that it's considered a big win if the ratings hold steady instead of dropping. Or if the pageant breaks even at the end of the year. Celebrating business practices that aim simply to stop the bleeding is a dreadful way to build—or even sustain—a company. And when you consider the reporting by reputable journalists from respected news organizations about contestants who are never able to collect their scholarships, scholarships that supposedly are the raison d'etre of the whole enterprise—well, good luck keeping those dollars coming in.

If Miss America is to survive, she will not survive because the Almighty God of Television somehow brought her enough viewers and advertisers in one particular year, or even in a string of years. She will not survive because she successfully panders to the lowest common denominator; this approach is antithetical not only to building a brand, but to crafting Miss America's brand in particular. Miss America will survive only if she decides exactly who she is, develops a lasting identity, and rejects the many temptations that run counter to that identity.

But before any of that can occur, the organization needs to get its act together. Stop rewarding mediocrity. Let go of staff members who have been promoted to their level of incompetence, or reassign them to jobs they can actually handle. Hire an outside firm to conduct an exhaustive institutional audit. Keep Children's Miracle Network around; it's a great group that does wonderful things. But stop balancing the books on the backs of kids with terminal illnesses. It's not only ethically reprehensible, it's borderline fraudulent. Most contestants would rather just pay an entry fee and be done with it. The Miss USA/Miss Universe entry-fee model actually means that the state directors who run the program make money (some of them a lot of money) and at the same time are held to a higher standard of professional accountability. Organize the former Miss Americas who want to be involved, and send them out as ambassadors with a specific marketing message. The pageant has spent almost a century creating strong, effective female leaders, but then it doesn't really do much with them aside from inviting them to the show each year. It's not only a waste of resources; it indicates that the people in charge don't even understand what the program accomplishes in the lives of very real women. Even more insidious, though, is that those who *do* try to effect positive change are systematically marginalized; the leadership has adopted a my-way-or-the-highway approach to running the pageant that hardly leaves any room for criticism. And as for transparency (chatty board members notwithstanding), it's about as rare as a size 16 Miss Texas.

Once again, Miss America is at a crossroads. Dealing with traditional expectations, damaging stereotypes, and outdated, conflicting ideas of who Miss America is and what she represents is no small task. It becomes even more daunting without clear leadership, vision, and strategy. If Miss America is to survive another hundred years, her caretakers must recognize and embrace contemporary American womanhood and how it is manifested in successive generations of contestants and viewers. There are many, many smart people on the sidelines who would love to help the organization evolve. Miss America will never again be what she once was. But it is still possible that she can become something greater than ever.

NOTES

TWO

p. 14. *It is a testament to her significance.* Hilary Levey Friedman, "There She Goes: A Trailblazing, Feminist Beauty Queen," *Huffington Post,* March 15, 2011; Sadie Stein, "A Miss America Who Took a Stand," *Jezebel* (blog), March 16, 2011.

p. 16. *"a 30-25-32 figure that was close to the flapper era ideal."* *New York Times,* October 5, 1995.

p. 17. *an RKO screen test.* Miss America Organization website (www.missamerica.org).

p. 17. *"the pageant was not on the up and up."* *Atlantic City Press,* September 11, 1933.

p. 17. *"entirely too much undue publicity."* Marian Bergeron, interview for *Miss America,* PBS American Experience/Orchard Films, 2002.

p. 18. *no money had been made by that year's pageant.* *Atlantic City Press,* September 11, 1933.

p. 18. *"Queen of American Beauty."* Miss America Organization website.

p. 18. *Fifty-two contestants.* Miss America Organization website.

p. 19. *"iron fist in a velvet glove."* Ric Ferentz, interview for *Miss America,* PBS American Experience/Orchard Films, 2002.

p. 19. *she was always referred to as "Miss Slaughter."* "Lenora Slaughter Frapart, the Doyenne of the American Beauty Pageant," *New York Press,* January 31, 2001.

p. 19. *"'First thing,' she explained."* "Lenora Slaughter Frapart," *New York Press.*

p. 20. *a high school dropout from Pittsburgh named Henrietta Leaver.* "Here's a Beauty Queen with No Hollywood Ambitions," *Pittsburgh Press,* August 14, 1935.

p. 20. *to create a nude sculpture of her.* "When the Sculptor Left Off the Bathing Suit," *Salt Lake City Tribune,* December 1, 1935.

p. 20. *since she had married during her year.* "Miss Leaver Honeymoons with Her Childhood Beau," *Pittsburgh Press,* July 18, 1936.

p. 20. *Bette still refuses to talk.* "1937: Bette Cooper," Miss America Organization website.

p. 21. *a $2,000 endorsement deal with a hat company.* "1930s—Decade in Review," Miss America Organization website.

p. 22. *"the Mayflower would have been seen as a plus."* Lisa Ades, director, *Miss America,* PBS American Experience/Orchard Films, 2002.

p. 23. *"Bess Myerson . . . or somebody else."* Ades, *Miss America.*

p. 23. *the Sholem Aleichem Cooperative Houses in the Bronx.* Wendy Wasserstein, "New York Stories: Hell's Kitchen Killers . . . Gotti and the Mob . . . and the Bess Mess," *New York Times* online, April 8, 1990.

p. 24. *I owed it to those women to give them a present.* Ades, *Miss America.*

p. 24. *"that I was first and foremost a Jew."* Emily D. Soloff, "Bess Myerson Reflects on Fame, Miss America and Judaism," *j: the Jewish News Weekly of Northern California* online, October 6, 1995. Originally published in *Chicago Jewish News.*

p. 24. *she remembers encountering anti-Semitism.* Soloff, "Bess Myerson Reflects on Fame."

p. 26. *"They accused me of making communist speeches."* Soloff, "Bess Myerson Reflects on Fame."

pp. 26–27. *to be crowned in a swimsuit.* "What's in a Name," the University of Memphis Centennial website (http://www.memphis.edu/centennial/bygone.htm).

p. 28. *"There was nothing but trouble from the minute that crown touched my head."* Owen Edwards, "American Idol," *Smithsonian Magazine* online, January 2006.

p. 28. *and crowned their winners in swimsuits.* Papers of Yolande

Betbeze, Miss America 1951: Overview of the Collection, Smithsonian Archives Center online (revised January 28, 2009).

p. 28. *the objectification of women in pageants.* Papers of Yolande Betbeze, Miss America 1951: Series 1, Miss America Reign, 1950–1951, 1994, undated.

p. 31. *"if it wasn't for Lenora."* Michael Yockel, "Lenora Slaughter Frapart, the Doyenne of the American Beauty Pageant," *New York Press*, January 31, 2001.

p. 32. *she legendarily "outtalked Billy Graham."* Frank Deford, *There She Is: The Life and Times of Miss America* (New York: Viking, 1971), 208.

FOUR

p. 39. *after their regularly scheduled programming but in time for the crowning.* A. R. Riverol, *Live from Atlantic City: A History of the Miss America Pageant* (Bowling Green, OH: Bowling Green State University Popular Press, 1992), 49–50.

p. 39. *a 39 share of the viewing audience.* Riverol, *Live From Atlantic City*, 56.

p. 41. *They become more beautiful with age.* Deford, *There She Is*, 107.

p. 41. *"order orange juice in a loud voice."* Deford, *There She Is*, 4.

SIX

p. 55. *every man, woman, and child in the United States of America.* Deford, *There She Is*, 194–196.

p. 57. *to permeate the perfect facades.* Deford, *There She Is*, 230.

p. 59. *no one in the ballroom had any idea what would happen next.* Claire Suddath, "The Day the Music Died," *Time* online, February 3, 2009.

pp. 60–61. *an image that oppresses women.* Robin Morgan, "No More Miss America!" redstockings.org., August 22, 1968.

p. 62. *had "nothing against homosexuals."* Mary Vespa, "Miss America, Tawny Godin, Puts a Ring on Her Finger and Steps on Some Toes," *People* online, March 22, 1976.

p. 62. *talking about her pet crab.* Deford, *There She Is*, 219.

p. 62. *the pageant was bumped from network television entirely.*

Bill Gorman, "Miss America Crowned: Whatever Happened to Beauty Pageants?" http:tvbythenumbers.zap2it.com.

EIGHT

p. 75. *dancing in a production number titled "Call Me 'Ms.'"* Ades, *Miss America*.

p. 79. *"the identity that TV stole from her in the first place."* Deford, *There She Is*, 197–198.

p. 80. *they had added a baby girl to their family.* Vanessa Williams biography, Biography.com.

p. 80. *the pageant's "There She Is" catchphrase.* Vanessa Williams, Helen Williams, and Irene Zutell, *You Have No Idea* (New York: Gotham Books, 2012), 75.

p. 80. *Arkansas's Lencola Sullivan became the first to finish in the top five.* Valerie Felita Kinloch, "The Rhetoric of Black Bodies," in *There She Is, Miss America: The Politics of Sex, Beauty, and Race in America's Most Famous Pageant*, ed. Elwood Watson and Darcy Martin (New York: Palgrave Macmillan, 2004), 99.

pp. 80–81. *the highly regarded musical theater program at Syracuse University.* Williams, Williams, and Zutell, *You Have No Idea*, 21.

p. 81. *So she decided to give it a go.* Williams, Williams, and Zutell, *You Have No Idea*, 22–23.

p. 81. *diversity was "alive and well."* Sarah Banet-Weiser, *The Most Beautiful Girl in the World: Beauty Pageants and National Identity* (Berkeley and Los Angeles: University of California Press, 1999), 129.

p. 84. *NAACP executive director Benjamin Hooks likened her to Jackie Robinson.* Banet-Weiser, *The Most Beautiful Girl in the World*, 123–124.

p. 84. *"They chose me because they thought I could do the job."* Banet-Weiser, *The Most Beautiful Girl in the World*, 132.

p. 85. *"I'd never take the stuff out—it was just too disgusting."* Williams, Williams, and Zutell, *You Have No Idea*, 32–33.

p. 85. *as she rode in her hometown parade.* Williams, 33.

p. 86. *remind anyone of that hard reality.* Gerald Early, "Waiting for Miss America," in *There She Is, Miss America*, 174–175.

p. 86. *and eventually sued* Penthouse *publisher Bob Guccione for printing them.* Williams, Williams, and Zutell, *You Have No Idea*, 67.

p. 86. *And there would not be a Miss America pageant today.* Ades, *Miss America.*

p. 87. *She was just the most verbal, bright, terrific seller.* Ades, *Miss America.*

p. 88. *more than $45,000 to that end.* Kate Kitchen, *The Strength of Grace* (Greensboro, NC: Eastman Press, 2004), 198.

p. 89. *"thirty-five to forty letters a day."* Kitchen, *The Strength of Grace*, 198.

p. 90. *or whether the crown was made of real diamonds.* Miss America Organization website (Kaye Lani Rae Rafko, 1988).

p. 90. *"speaking out on the need for more nurses."* Jeff Meade, "Kaye Lani: I Just Wanted to Be Me," *Monroe Evening News*, September 15, 2007.

p. 90. *my own hospice center for all terminally ill patients.* William Goldman, *Hype and Glory* (New York: Villard Books, 1990), 295–296.

p. 90. *complications after a heart attack.* "Albert A. Marks, Jr." http://www.findagrave.com.

NINE

p. 96. *"winningest coach in the history of national collegiate debate."* Wendy Leopold, "Scott Deatherage, Longtime Debate Coach, Dies at 47," Northwestern University website, December 30, 2009.

p. 108. *Instead of serving us a consumer culture icon of loveliness.* James Carroll, "A Beautiful Face on AIDS," *Boston Globe*, May 26, 1998.

TEN

p. 114. *Jeff Margolis took over as both producer and director.* "About," http.jeffmargolisproductions.com.

p. 115. *the most painfully detailed account of that night's events.* Goldman, *Hype and Glory*, 276–297.

p. 117. *"they have to look and act like their peers."* Kari Huus, "Miss America Seeks Relevance and Ratings," NBC News online, September 17, 2004.

p. 117. *the crowning moment at the end of the show.* Huus, "Miss America Seeks Relevance."

p. 120. *"more than a mere beauty queen."* Banet-Weiser, *The Most Beautiful Girl in the World*, 43.

p. 120. *"when you've got this thing on top of your head?"* Michelle Tauber et al., "American Beauties: 80 Years," *People* online, October 16, 2000.

p. 121. *it should be eliminated from the judging criteria.* Tauber et al., "American Beauties."

p. 121. *"the so-called experts."* Sarah Overstreet, "Miss America's Swimsuit? So What?" *Seattle Times* online, September 1, 1990.

p. 121. *thumbs-up to the swimsuit competition.* Bonnie J. Dow, "Forum: Feminism, Miss America, and Media Mythology," *Rhetoric & Public Affairs* 6 no. 1 (2003): 140.

p. 122. *a memorably itsy-bitsy yellow version.* Stewart Mason, ALLMUSIC (allmusic.com), "Brian Hyland: Itsy Bitsy Teenie Weenie Yellow Polka Dot Bikini."

p. 123. *"permitted to visit casinos."* Mildred Brick et al., "Mrs. John D. Feehan, The Sixth Chairman," *Miss America National Hostess Committee: 1937–2000* (unpublished), p. 2.

p. 123. *"They listened because of that fake crown."* Tauber et al., "American Beauties."

p. 124. *"So don't talk to me about two-piece swimsuits."* Bill Kent, "Mr. Miss America," *New York Times* online, September 13, 1998.

p. 124. *no cash reserve at the beginning of his term.* Elaine Rose, "Miss America CEO Stepping Down," *The Press of Atlantic City,* July 14, 1998, A4.

TWELVE

p. 141. *"the Miss America Pageant's Pygmalion."* Ellen O'Brien and Mike Schurman, "Albert Marks, Miss American Leader," *Philadelphia Inquirer,* September 25, 1989.

p. 145. *"a passive beauty queen to a motivated social activist."* Rose, "Miss America CEO Stepping Down."

p. 145. *six-member search committee that interviewed the candidates.* Rose, "Miss America CEO Stepping Down."

p. 146. *"looking forward to training his replacement."* Rose, "Miss America CEO Stepping Down."

p. 148. *enforcement of certain clauses.* Elaine Rose, "Miss A Squabbles Will Stay in the Public Eye," *The Press of Atlantic City,* March 8, 2002.

p. 149. *Beck was fired two weeks after the crowning.* Rose, "Miss A Squabbles."

p. 149. *a defendant in the case.* Rose, "Miss A Squabbles."

p. 150. *awarded Beck $80,000 in severance pay.* "Offstage Archive: People on PNB January–March 2003," Pageant News Bureau (website).

p. 150. *not a deal breaker for the pageant.* Michael Klein, "Talking with Robert Renneisen: Miss America Made a Believer of Him," *Philadelphia Inquirer* online, July 23, 2000.

p. 151. *"their perceptions can be changed forever."* Klein, "Talking with Robert Renneisen."

p. 152. *"a pleading letter from her Miss America handlers."* Steve Rubenstein, "A Goodwill Visit from Filipina Miss America: Honolulu Teacher in S.F. to Dispel Title's Myths," *San Francisco Chronicle*, November 9, 2000.

p. 152. *the staff grew to include.* Mildred Brick et al., "Mrs. Corinne J. Sparenberg, The Seventh Chairman," *Miss America National Hostess Committee: 1937–2000* (unpublished), p. 4.

p. 152. *In 2000, total functional expenses were.* "Miss America Organization in Linwood, NJ," http://www.faqs.org/tax-exempt/NJ/Miss-America-Organization.html.

p. 152. *"the money that the pageant had is being thrown away."* Oliver Poole, "Miss America Competition Faces Bankruptcy Threat," *Telegraph*, April 14, 2002, www.telegraph.co.uk.

p. 154. *ultimately the pageant did not get the requested funding.* Alex Kuczynski, "State Pageants at War with Miss America Organization," *New York Times*, February 16, 2002.

p. 154. *it had actually been Renneisen himself.* Jake Tapper, "Brains 1, Barbie 0," *Salon*, September 25, 2002.

p. 155. *post-crowning party at the Trump Taj Mahal.* Tapper, "Brains 1, Barbie 0."

p. 155. *"get the hell out' of the Miss America organization."* Steven V. Cronin, "States Say Renneisen Fired First Shot," *Press of Atlantic City*, February 14, 2002.

p. 155. *"They normally suffer in silence."* Cronin, "States Say Renneisen Fired First Shot."

p. 157. *"trying to put it all in Katie's mouth."* Kuczynski, "State Pageants at War with Miss America Organization."

p. 158. *the "many masters" the executive was obligated to please.* Steven V. Cronin, "Miss A Pageant Holds Out for a Hero," *Press of Atlantic City*, March 3, 2002.

p. 159. *"a modern, transparent enterprise that is run openly, pro-*

fessionally, and peacefully?" "More Miss America Turmoil: Time for Change," *Press of Atlantic City*, March 3, 2002.

p. 159. *the board appointed vice president George Bauer.* Cronin, "Miss A Pageant Holds Out for a Hero."

p. 159. *"and I'm going to tap into it."* Cronin, "Miss A Pageant Holds Out for a Hero."

p. 160. *"refused to return phone calls to both contractors and major sponsors."* Elaine Rose, "Contractor Joins Complaints about Miss A Organization," *Press of Atlantic City*, February 14, 2002.

p. 161. *tremendous animosity from the public.* Michael Pritchard, "Miss A Taking Heat from Locals after Money Push," *Press of Atlantic City*, December 21, 2001.

p. 161. *there were those who felt a shakedown was happening.* Pritchard, "Miss A Taking Heat from Locals after Money Push."

p. 161. *rather cheap swipe at Rob Beck.* Steven V. Cronin, "Pageant, Miss A Say the Honeymoon Was Never Sour," *Press of Atlantic City*, February 16, 2002.

p. 162. *resign her position as Miss North Carolina 2002.* Katherine Seigenthaler, "Miss America Pageant Still Suffers Fatal Flaws," *Chicago Tribune*, August 7, 2002.

p. 163. *"Begin-and-Sadat style."* Tapper, "Brains 1, Barbie 0."

p. 163. *the pageant essentially kicked Revels to the curb.* "Original Miss N.C. Loses Tiara Tug of War," *Good Morning America*, September 13, 2002.

p. 163. *she had still been reinstated in North Carolina.* "Original Miss N.C. Loses Tiara Tug of War."

p. 163. *claims that she was illegally barred from taking part.* Nancy McCleary, "Thieves Take Pageant Crowns from Former Miss North Carolina," *Fayetteville Observer*, January 28, 2011.

p. 163. *in the parade of former titleholders on its website.* "Miss North Carolina: History," http://missnc.org/?page_id=14.

p. 164. *ultimately deciding on Harvard.* "Abstinence Advocate Is New Miss America!" *Eagle Forum: Education Reporter*, October 2, 2002, no. 201.

p. 165. *"making proper sexual decisions."* John W. Kennedy, "Erika Harold: Miss America for Such a Time as This," *Pentecostal Evangel*, 2003.

p. 165. *future assets to her stated plans to run for public office.* "Abstinence Rally Rocks Chicago," *Eagle Forum: Education Reporter*, January 1999, no. 156.

p. 165. *"pooled money to buy a gun and kill her."* Kate Shindle, "Virgin with a Vengeance," *POZ*, May 2003.

p. 167. *asserted that she was "being muzzled."* George Archibald, "Pageant Permits Promotion of Chastity: Miss America Now Free to Tout Issue," *Washington Times*, October 10, 2002.

p. 167. *"promote the healthy message of abstinence until marriage."* Lara Riscol, "Miss America's Stealth Virginity Campaign," *Salon*, October 28, 2002.

p. 168. *"went out of her way to hide any information about abstinence."* Shindle, "Virgin with a Vengeance."

p. 168. *the relationship between teen sexual activity and youth violence.* Archibald, "Pageant Permits Promotion of Chastity."

p. 169. *"And that woman is Erika Harold."* Tapper, "Brains 1, Barbie 0."

p. 169. *a generally unflattering piece about the pageant.* Olivia Barker, "Miss America and Me, the '52nd Contestant.'" *USA Today*, September 19, 2002.

p. 171. *or contestants struggle to collect the scholarships they've won.* Jennifer 8. Lee, "Winners Cite Broken Promises in Pageants," *New York Times*, September 24, 2007.

p. 171. *Local winners across the country have threatened legal action.* Lee, "Winners Cite Broken Promises in Pageants."

p. 173. *"Don't mess with it."* Jason Spencer, "Judge Alleges Unethical Behavior at Miss SC," *Spartanburg Herald Journal*, July 7, 2010.

p. 173. *Sanders and his wife, Gail, were "retiring."* Linda Conley, "Sanders Retiring after 50 Years as Miss SC Director," *Spartanburg Herald Journal*, July 11, 2010.

p. 174. *"We'll be happy to look into it."* Spencer, "Judge Alleges Unethical Behavior."

THIRTEEN

p. 182. *"Miss America must continue to appear ten times a year."* Jeffrey Gettleman, "There She Isn't: Miss America Pageant Leaves Atlantic City," *New York Times*, August 26, 2005.

p. 186. *TLC wants to pay less to televise the show.* Oskar Garcia, "TLC Drops Miss America Pageant," *Huffington Post*, March 1, 2010.

p. 188. *"She has performed in a prison!"* "Leigh-Taylor Smith on Miss America—Kerrigan-Lowdermilk's Say the Word," Kerrigan-

Lowdermilk (video: http://www.youtube.com/watch?v=b5VUyAq8 Bqw).

p. 189. *one young lady after another, assembly-line style.* "Pageant Confidential: The Road to Miss America," *20/20* (video: http://www .youtube.com/watch?v=LNbdsdVBcMU).

p. 190. *applying the glue itself is "an art."* Ellie Krupnick, "Miss America Beauty Secrets: Butt Glue and Lots of Tape," *Huffington Post,* January 11, 2013.

FOURTEEN

p. 196. *ABC paid a reported $5.6 million.* Michael Schneider, "ABC Gets Back with Miss America," *Variety,* May 23, 2010.

p. 198. *anti-bullying and self-esteem initiatives.* "Miss Teen USA: Charities," http://www.missuniverse.com/missteenusa/charities /index.

p. 198. *her work with AIDS charities on NBC's* Today. "Meet the New Miss Universe," *Today* (video), August 26, 2010.

p. 198. *a number of other HIV/AIDS specific organizations.* "Miss Universe 2012 Olivia Culpo Returns to AID FOR AIDS," editorial, aidforaids.com, April 8, 2013.

p. 199. *an HIV-positive child fostered by her family.* "Miss America's AIDS Platform: Making It Personal," FoxNews.com: Infectious, April 9, 2010.

p. 199. *"and the girl can sing!!"* Roxanne Roberts and Amy Argetsinger, "Miss America Judge Rush Limbaugh: Miss VA 'Has It All,'" *Washington Post,* February 1, 2010.

p. 199. *an AIDS volunteer at age nine.* Macy L. Freeman, "Miss America Headlines Conference at Howard in Personal Campaign Against HIV," Howard University News Service, November 15, 2010.

p. 199. *Miss America 1971, Phyllis George.* "American Signature, Inc., to Debut the Miss America Youth Collection," Miss America: Press Releases, October 14, 2010.

p. 200. *a World AIDS Day conference at Howard University.* Freeman, "Miss America Headlines Conference."

p. 201. *"where the Miss America pageant belongs."* Wayne Parry, "Atlantic City Welcomes Home Miss America Pageant," ap.org., February 14, 2013.

p. 202. *Don Wadsworth . . . made it happen.* Parry, "Atlantic City Welcomes Home."

p. 202. *Casino Reinvestment Development Authority.* Jennifer Bogdan, "Miss America Pageant Will Get $7.3M to Return to Atlantic City," *Press of Atlantic City,* April 15, 2013.

p. 202. *asserting that the price was too low.* "Lender Says He Won't Approve Sale of Atlantic City Trump Plaza," Associated Press, April 23, 2013.

p. 203. *spread over a three-year contract.* Bogdan, "Miss America Pageant Will Get $7.3M."

p. 203. *both of whom work to stop child sexual abuse.* Miss America Organization, "Two Miss Americas to Speak on Child Abuse Tuesday," April 23, 2013. Via e-mail.

p. 205. *"worthy of his Hollywood roots."* Jennifer Bogdan, "Miss America's Finances Fluctuate, Records Show," *The Press of Atlantic City,* February 8, 2014.

ACKNOWLEDGMENTS

This one really did take a village; I'm grateful to all those who contributed stories, memories, details, photos, and the various other types of fuel that propel a writer toward the finish line.

It's fair to say that without Mark Crispin Miller, this book probably wouldn't have gotten off the ground. After I spoke in one of his NYU classes, Mark encouraged me, strategized with me, pitched me to the higher-ups, and helped me to shape the story of Miss America as I have lived it. Thank you for having confidence in a rookie nonfiction writer, and for guiding me to the University of Texas Press.

Speaking of UT, I would have been lost without the patience, diligence, and vision of Robert Devens, Lynne Chapman, Sarah Rosen, Jan McInroy, and their terrific team in Austin. They pushed, they advised, and they inspired me to improve upon what was already on the page.

Thanks also to my literary agent, Laurie Liss, who has been an awesome advocate and guide for me, and is just generally an all-around cool chick. And to the various other agents and managers in my life, thank you for understanding when I needed to batten down the hatches and turn down offers.

To those who generously provided photos, without hesitation, and without even having a complete manuscript to read: Vicki Gold Levi, Bob Ruffolo, Kaye Lani Rae Rafko, Don Kravitz, and Daryl Schabinger, I am indebted to you.

Thanks to Doug Wert, a tireless champion who has always been in my corner.

Thank you to whichever genius decided to run train tracks through the Adirondack Mountains; Amtrak's round trips to Montreal were often the only way for me to escape the craziness of a million other projects and focus on this one . . . even if the border patrol guards thought I was a little crazy.

This book would not have been possible without those who guided me through the Miss America experience: the "Dream Team" in Chicago, my traveling companions, Marilyn and John Feehan (and all the rest of the amazing volunteers who showed me what Miss America can be and encouraged me to see it through), and the countless contestants and other Miss Americas who have inspired me more than they know.

Finally, thanks to you, the reader. This is one person's interpretation, through a single lens, and based on a specific set of experiences. Clearly, there are many others. But I appreciate that you took the time to consider mine.

INDEX